Discovering the Entrepreneur Within
Understanding the Entrepreneurial Process

Preliminary Edition

Robert F. Sinclair
Governors State University

Kendall Hunt
publishing company

Cover image © Anatoly Maslennikov/Shutterstock.com
Interior images © Shutterstock.com

Kendall Hunt
publishing company

www.kendallhunt.com
Send all inquiries to:
4050 Westmark Drive
Dubuque, IA 52004-1840

Copyright © 2014 by Kendall Hunt Publishing Company

ISBN 978-1-4652-1621-2

All rights reserved. No part of this publication may be reproduced,
stored in a retrieval system, or transmitted, in any form or by any means,
electronic, mechanical, photocopying, recording, or otherwise,
without the prior written permission of the copyright owner.

Printed in the United States of America

Because there are too many people to thank properly here (and you already know you have my undying gratitude), I would like to dedicate this book to the person who truly made any of this possible...

I miss you mom

TABLE OF CONTENTS

PREFACE (WHY SHOULD YOU BELIEVE ANYTHING I SAY?) .... **VIII**

   The Need for this Book ix
   Biography x
      Ph.D. in Entrepreneurship from the "School of Hard Knocks" x
      Academic Ph.D. in Entrepreneurship from the University of Louisville xvi
      Summary of My Qualifications xx
      What This Book Offers xxi
      What This Book Is Not xxii
      Why the Book Is Written the Way It Is xxii

SECTION 1: A GENERAL OVERVIEW OF ENTREPRENEURSHIP **1**

CHAPTER 1: WHAT EXACTLY IS ENTREPRENEURSHIP **3**

   Entrepreneurship—Misconceptions 4
      Misconception: Entrepreneurs are Gamblers 4
      Misconception: Starting a Business is Entrepreneurship 5
      Misconception: Small Business and Entrepreneurship are the same 6
      Misconception: Once an Entrepreneur, Always an Entrepreneur 7
      Misconception: Entrepreneurs—Are they Born or Made? 8
   Entrepreneurship—the Intersection of Entrepreneur and Opportunity 11
      Entrepreneurial Mindset 11
      Motivation to Action 13
      Opportunity 13
   Summary 16

CHAPTER 2: THE NEED FOR ENTREPRENEURSHIP **17**

   The Entrepreneur: an Agent for Change 18
   Entrepreneurship and the Business Environment 20
      Economic Growth 20
      Employment Growth 22
      Employee-Employer Loyalty 23
   Entrepreneurship and the Economy 24
      Industrial Economies 25
      Incremental Innovations 25
      Entrepreneurial Economies 27
      Radical Innovations 28
   Summary 29

CHAPTER 3: THE EQUIFINAL NATURE OF ENTREPRENEURSHIP ... 33

Entrepreneurial Pathways ... 34
No Entrepreneurial Intentions ... 34
Low Entrepreneurial Intentions ... 36
Moderate Entrepreneurial Intentions ... 37
Strong Entrepreneurial Intentions ... 40

Summary ... 42

CHAPTER 4: THE DIFFERING FORMS OF ENTREPRENEURSHIP ... 43

Forms of Entrepreneurship ... 44
Orignation Entrepreneurship ... 44
Orignation Entrepreneurship Summary ... 49
Corporate Entrepreneurship ... 49
Corporate Entrepreneurship Summary ... 53
Commerial Entrepreneurship ... 53
Develpomental Entrepreneurship ... 54
Misconception: Entrepreneurship is a Perminate State ... 56
Social Entrepreneurship ... 57
Misconceptions about Social Entrepreneurship: Non-profit ... 58
Misconceptions about Social Entrepreneurship: Charity ... 59

SECTION 2: THE ENTREPRENEUR ... 61

Measure your Entrepreneurial Mindset ... 63
Understanding the Entrepreneurial Process ... 64

CHAPTER 5: ENTREPRENEURIAL MINDSET ... 69

Mindset ... 70
Entrepreneurial Mindset ... 71
Creating an Entrepreneurial Mindset ... 72
Knowledge of Entrepreneurship ... 72
Belief in One's Ability to Become an Entrepreneur ... 73
    Entity Schemas ... 73
        Static Entity Schema ... 74
        Dynamic Entity Schema ... 75
    Possible Entrepreneurial Self-Concept ... 77
        Intellectual Self ... 78
        Social Self ... 79
        Emotional Self ... 79
        Physical Self ... 80
    Entrepreneurial Self-Efficacy ... 82
        Prior Experience ... 83
        Observed Experience ... 84
        Social Persuasion ... 85

Chapter 6: Creativity and Innovation ... 87

What is Creativity and Innovation and how do they differ? ... 88
Why does it matter what form I choose? ... 88
- *Creativity* ... 89
- *Innovation* ... 90

What psychological techniques can we use to restart our creativity? ... 95
- *Counterfactual Thinking* ... 96
- *Divergent Thinking* ... 98
- *Conceptual Blending* ... 99

Additional tips to help improve one's creativity ... 100
- *Make time* ... 100
- *Find a quiet space* ... 101
- *Free your mind* ... 102
- *Sleep can be your friend* ... 103
- *Write it down* ... 104
- *Be observant* ... 105
- *Learn something new every day* ... 105

Chapter 7: Psychological Hardiness and the Entrepreneur ... 106

Psychological Hardiness ... 107
How does psychological hardiness work? ... 107
- *Commitment* ... 108
- *Control* ... 110
  - *Cognitive Control* ... 111
  - *Decisional Control* ... 112
  - *Behavioral Control* ... 113
- *Challenge* ... 115

Chapter 8: Ethics and the Entrepreneur ... 117

What are Ethics? ... 118
The Need for Ethics in Entrepreneurship ... 118
- *"I Had No Choice"* ... 119
- *"Absolute Power Corrupts Absolutely"* ... 123

Avoiding Ethical Dilemmas ... 126
- *Determine your Values* ... 127

Preventing Unethical Behavior ... 130
- *Checks and Balances* ... 130

SECTION 3: NASCENT ENTREPRENEURSHIP 133

CHAPTER 9: LOCATING AND CREATING ENTREPRENEURIAL OPPORTUNITIES 136

- **Locating and Creating Entrepreneurial Opportunities** 137
- **Opportunity Alertness** 137
- **Constrained Systematic Search** 140
  - *Knowledge* 141
  - *Specific Knowledge* 142
  - *Information Channels* 143
  - *Consideration Set* 144
  - *Signals* 145
- **Opportunity Conversion** 146

CHAPTER 10: EVALUATING OPPORTUNITIES 150

- **Opportunity Fit** 151
- **Confirmation Bias** 152
- **Determining Monetary Value-Fit** (Feasibility) 153
  - *Creating an Objective Measure of Profit Potential* 153
  - *Estimating the Monetary Value of an Opportunity* 156
- **Determining Personal-Knowledge Fit** (Feasibility) 160
- **Determining Personal-Value Fit** (Desirability) 162
- **Determining Family-Value Fit** (Desirability) 163
- **Overall Evaluation** (Opportunity Score) 165

APPENDIX A: EXERCISES 167

- Exercise 1: Interview with an Entrepreneur 169
- Exercise 2: The Value of an Entrepreneurial Economy 171
- Exercise 3: Describe Which Path Is Right for You 173
- Exercise 4: Which Form of Entrepreneurship Is Right for You? 175
- Exercise 5: Forming Your Entrepreneurial Mindset 177
- Exercise 6: Creativity and Innovation 179
- Exercise 7: Psychological Hardiness 181
- Exercise 8: Entrepreneurial Ethics 183
- Exercise 9: Locating and Creating Opportunities 185
- Exercise 10: Evaluating Opportunities 187

Preface

The Need for this Book

It is my opinion that the first question people should ask themselves before buying any book of this type is, *"why do I need it?"* Obviously, if you are considering this book you are interested in or curious about entrepreneurship. However, the next question you should be asking is, *"why this book and not one of the many others written on this topic?"*—**good question.**

Far too often entrepreneurship is thought of as just "starting a new business." Let me tell you the topic is far more complex than that. In fact, believe it or not, starting a new business may not even be considered entrepreneurship—but we'll talk more about that later. Because many of the books written on the subject of entrepreneurship tend to focus on what entrepreneurs do and on the different aspects of starting a business, I feel they fail to include many of the basic things you really need to know. Most importantly, *"how do I do it?"* Knowing what entrepreneurs do is not the same as knowing how they do it. This book focuses on the entrepreneurial process. It describes exactly what entrepreneurship is and is not. It describes what entrepreneurs do that is different from other people, and most importantly, how you can become an entrepreneur if you so choose.

Throughout this book, topics are based on information you need to know in order to become an entrepreneur. This information is supported with years of academic research and personal examples designed to help you personalize the material and thus truly understand the different topics. When you complete this book, you will not only understand what entrepreneurship really is, more importantly, you will know that you can be an entrepreneur if you choose and how you will do it.

Now that you understand why this book is the right one for you, you should be asking one more question, *"how do I know this author is the right person to explain the entrepreneurial process?"* —**great question!**

Preface

Biography

My name is Robert Sinclair, and as much as I hate to talk about myself (it feels like bragging), I understand the importance of knowing who you are learning from and how they know what they know. How else can you be sure that you are learning from someone who truly knows what they are talking about? Well, I am fond of saying that I have two Ph.D.'s (Doctor of Philosophy), one from the "School of Hard Knocks" and the other from the University of Louisville. Most importantly, I have been an entrepreneur all of my life.

Ph.D. in Entrepreneurship from the "School of Hard Knocks"

I began my first Ph.D. (from the "School of Hard Knocks") as a corporate entrepreneur in 1978 at the age of 16 working for a fast food company. At this time I had no idea what an entrepreneur was or any clue that I was one. All I knew was that things at this company were very inefficient. I could see several ways that the owner could save money and thought if I helped him, I could use this opportunity to get more money as a reward. Before I knew it I was a delivery boy, cook, repairman, and a supervisor for his three different restaurants. The problem I ended up with was that I was working 60-hour weeks, for minimum wage, and I got separate paychecks from each of his three businesses (so he didn't have to pay me overtime, which I didn't know at the time was illegal) all the while attending high school full time. Although I was being taken advantage of, I made good money for a kid, had a fancy car, money enough to do most things that I wanted, and job security (what other sucker was he going to get to work this hard for no overtime?). By the time I was 18 I had streamlined his business processes, graduated from high school, and was looking for something more.

My next job was working for a foundry in Detroit, Michigan making car parts. The first day was crazy. I went in and asked for the supervisor, he handed me a pair of gloves and a set of pliers and proceeded to walk me over to a machine the size of a school bus. He started it up and said, "When the machine opens up, take the parts out and put them in this tank of liquid," then he walked away. What he didn't tell me was the parts coming out of the machine were 375°. Half an hour later, he came back and said, *"What the heck are you doing?"* (O.K., maybe it was a little bit more colorful than that). *"Haven't you ever done this before?"* Well, not only had I never done it before, I had never even seen the inside of a factory before. You see, I knew the girlfriend of the owner's son and she talked him into hiring me. He proceeded to show me how to take the part out of this beast of a machine using the pliers and told me "You won't last the week. It takes years to learn how to do this job and no one here is going to waste the time to teach you." Well to an entrepreneur, *"those are fighting words"* (figuratively of course). I proceeded to ask questions of anyone who would talk to me. Instead of taking a lunch or other breaks, I would watch other people run their machines, and just kept trying different things to see what did and didn't work. Within six months I was not only able to run any machine they put me on, but I was able to run more parts in eight hours than almost anyone else. Before I knew it, the other operators were coming to *me* with questions. Honestly, that challenge was probably the best thing that happened to me. If that supervisor hadn't told me I could not do it, I most likely would have quit within the first week. It was extremely hard work, and although I was making good money (twice minimum wage), I was still only 18 after all, and truthfully, a bit on the lazy side.

A few years later, although I was succeeding at this latest job, something my father told me kept going through my head, *"Work smart, not hard,"* and I was working quite hard for the money I was making. For that reason, I set my eyes on a front office job. There I could make the same amount of money, or more, and from what it looked like to me, I'd hardly have to work at all. Thus, when a job for an estimator position opened up, I applied. An estimator is a person who takes a blueprint of a brand new part and determines how much it will cost to produce it, how much it will cost to build the tools needed to make it, and how much money the company can charge the customer for the final product. The next day the owner called me into the office and said, *"Rob, I like you but you're not qualified for this job. You need a college degree and years of experience."* Again, like most entrepreneurs, I asked one simple question—**why**. He laughed and said, *"It takes an understanding of the entire manufacturing process, the ability to read a blueprint, calculate part weights, figure out the most effective way to manufacture the part, and the ability to calculate how much it is going to cost to produce."* I responded with *"so what's the problem?"* He laughed again. I went on to explain that I could read blueprints, I had taken four years of drafting in high school and was always at the top of my drafting classes. I understood the entire manufacturing process at his company and had offered suggestions on several occasions for improvements, many of which he had already adopted. The rest I explained was knowledge he would likely have to teach anyone he hired anyway, so why not me. I topped it off with one final question (one I already knew the answer to), *"Did you go to college?"* You see, I knew he had not. He ended our conversation with, *"I'll think about it."* I responded with, *"Thank you, that's all I'm asking for."*

After two weeks of waiting, and watching the company interview people for the job with no word, I realized they were not really even considering me for the job. I knew that if I didn't do something soon I was going to be stuck in my current position forever. All of the men in my family worked for General Motors, and although GM had not been hiring for almost 10 years, I learned from my family that GM was about to hire for a brand new plant in Pontiac, Michigan. It was a job working on the line but I figured it is better than the dead end job I was in so I applied. A week later I was called into GM for an interview and to my surprise was scheduled for a physical the next week. I had two weeks' vacation saved up, so I took my vacation time with the intent of turning in my notice as soon as I got the final word from GM. Well, the word must have gotten out to my boss, no surprise since the owner's son and I shared several friends, and two days into my vacation the owner of the company showed up at my front door. This was a shock. I didn't know he even knew where I lived. He asked to come in, we sat down and he cut right to the chase. *"So I hear you're leaving us."* Stunned, I told him the truth. I was most likely going to take a job with GM. I went on to tell him that I really appreciated all that he had done for me and assured him that I would give him at least two weeks' notice. To my surprise, he offered me the office job if I would stay. Although it was less money and way worse benefits than I would have gotten from GM, I accepted. I figured at least with him I now had a chance to make a future. After all, he came to me. If he was willing to go out of his way to come to my home, and talk to me personally, he must see a future for me too (maybe he saw the entrepreneur in me).

This story is typical of how I managed to push my way up the corporate ladder, first estimator, then assistant production manager, then production manager, and finally operations manager. The way I did it was by being a corporate entrepreneur. I went into every new job and learned everything I could about everything going on at the company. I looked for ways to improve and streamline the process, and in doing so, made myself a valued asset to the company. The problem was I was making significantly less money than most people doing the same jobs at other companies were. I eventually learned that doing it this way could only get me so far up the company ladder. You see, when you get to upper management there is no one above you from which to learn. This was the first time I understood why college was so important. Yes, many entrepreneurs have managed to become successful without a college education. However, I can tell you from firsthand experience they worked ten times harder and made far more mistakes along the way than they needed to. If fact, it is my opinion that the lack of a proper education in entrepreneurship is a major contributing factor as to why so many entrepreneurs fail the first several times they try (but I am getting ahead of myself. We will talk about this in detail later in the book).

Eventually, I realized I had hit the glass ceiling. You see, often in the business world what looks like a clear path to the top ends with an abrupt stop you did not see coming, thus the term glass ceiling. While most people stop and accept they have risen as high in the business world as they can, I began to look for a way to get around it. In 1994, that chance came. The company I was then working for was having an extremely difficult time finding another company to machine a line of parts we needed for a major automotive company. We went to every company within 100 miles and no one could do a consistently good job machining these parts, and were on the verge of losing one of our major customers. Fortunately, I knew what the problem was. Virtually all of the companies we had tried had automated their machining processes and what this line of parts needed was the human touch. Unfortunately, after these companies had spent millions of dollars updating their machining process, and let hundreds of people go, they were not willing to take on a job their automated machines could not handle. I knew that I could start a company to machine these parts by hand and do a consistently good job. I also knew that I would need at least $10,000 and six months to do it. But we didn't have that kind of time to work with. So, like most people, I sat and did nothing. This is because the entrepreneur in me had become dormant. I had a good paying job, a wife and young children, and had decided to become a small business entrepreneur later in life. That is, until one day the owner walked into my office and closed the door. He said, *"Rob, if we don't do something about this machining problem, we are going to lose this customer and if that happens, we are in real trouble."* So I explained to him the problem as I saw it. I went on to tell him that if I had the time and the money, I knew I could start a company to do the part the way we needed but we just did not have that kind of time. This was on a Wednesday. The next morning I went into my office and within 15 minutes the owner was there. He handed me a check for $10,000 and said, *"There is a truck full of parts at the machining company. Call the driver and tell him where to deliver them. I need 2000 pair by Monday or the customer is pulling all their work from us. Do what you have to do and we'll work out the details later."* Finally, I had found my chance to move from a corporate entrepreneur to a small business entrepreneur.

Now some might say, *"You're just lucky."*—**I could not disagree more**. When it comes to my accomplishments, I do not believe in luck. I believe in being prepared to take advantage of almost any situation should the opportunity arise—**entrepreneurship**. I proceeded to call my wife and tell her I was starting a business—today. I called the driver and gave him directions to my house. I then called everyone I knew and asked if they wanted a job. Surprisingly, everyone turned me down (something we will also discuss in further detail later. It's not as easy as you think to get employees when you are starting an entrepreneurial venture), nevertheless, most agreed to do as much as they could to help me get started. I left work and went to a hardware store and bought every tool I could lay my hands on that might have any chance of doing the job I needed to accomplish, and went home to get started. To save you all the painful, sleepless details, come Monday morning I delivered 1000 pair of parts to the customer and waited to hear the bad news (I had failed). To my surprise, the inspector looked at the parts and said, *"Well it's about time. I am tired of all the junk you have been sending us. You must have finally found a company that understands what we need. How soon can you get us the rest of the* *parts?"* After telling her a couple of days, I went back to my car and quietly said to myself, *"We did it. We actually did it."* Two years later, I had 22 employees, a 6000-sq ft building, and was doing $1,000,000 a year in sales. The problem now was boredom. You see, what I did not realize at the time was that I am a *serial entrepreneur*. Serial entrepreneurs enjoy the challenge of starting new ventures. Once the venture becomes a regular business, they lose interest in the day-to-day running of the company. I love the unknown that comes with starting an entrepreneurial venture. The getting up in the morning with no idea what adventure that day will hold. I don't like the day-to-day running of a business. I find I am much happier leaving that to others. Anyway, by this time in my life, I had already started two companies and was looking for a third entrepreneurial opportunity when it hit me, *"Why not help other people start their own companies?"* I had never heard of an entrepreneurial consultant (nor had anyone else I talked to at the time), but it seemed like this could be a way to stay involved in the start-up process indefinitely. Thus ended my Ph.D. from the "School of Hard Knocks" and began my academic Ph.D.

Academic Ph.D. in Entrepreneurship from the University of Louisville

In 2001 I sold or closed my businesses. I was 38, divorced, and was trying to figure out the best way to become an entrepreneurial consultant. In April I was checking out colleges for my oldest daughter. She was about to graduate high school and, based on what I had learned about trying to make it in the world without a college education, she was getting a degree in something no matter what. I didn't even care in what, all I knew was she was not going to struggle as hard as I had due to a lack of education. I was checking out Central Michigan University (CMU) when I jokingly told the woman at the registrar's office that, if I had it all to do over again, *"I would have gone to college here."* You see, I had been accepted at CMU exactly 20 years earlier, but at that time had decided college was not for me. No one in my family had ever gone to college and none of them really saw much value in it. Moreover, I was broke, so when I received that job offer in Detroit we talked about earlier, I decided to go that route instead. After I told her this, the woman got a funny look on her face and said, *"Do you have a minute?"* I said sure and she disappeared into the back. Fifteen minutes later she returned and asked me, *"Have you ever attended any other institution of higher education in the past 20 years?"* I replied, *"No."* She went on to state that I was still a registered student and because I had never attended any other institution of higher education, technically, my entrance date had simply been deferred. In short, all I had to do was write a letter explaining my intent to start. I was stunned. I had never even considered college as an option at this point in my life; after all, I was 38, not some 18 year old.

I thought about it for a couple of days and the more I thought about it the more it made sense. I had a wealth of experience as an entrepreneur, but I knew from experience that people feel more comfortable if you have a formal education. By this time, my oldest daughter had decided to attend CMU that fall. I decided to ask her what she thought. After all, what kid wants to be going to the same college at the same time as their father? I resolved that if it made her uncomfortable, even a little, I wouldn't do it (I know now that was just an excuse not to do it). Her response shocked me. She said, *"I don't care. You are going into business, right?"* She went on to say that even though she was not sure what she was going to major in, she knew it was not going to be business. That meant that we would likely never see each other anyway; that is, unless we wanted to. She said, *"If it makes you happy, you should do it."* I didn't know what to say so I just said, *"I'll have to think about it."* With that, I looked at my finances and realized that I could manage it, if I could complete the degree in three years. I looked into CMU further and found that they were the only college in the state of Michigan at the time that offered a bachelor's degree in entrepreneurship—perfect. After looking at the requirements it seemed to me that if I went full-time, including summers, and took at least 21 credits each semester, I could complete the degree in two and a half years. This gave me six months to start my entrepreneurial consulting business before I was in trouble financially. Truthfully, I just couldn't find a good reason to say no. In May of 2001 I became a 38-year-old college freshman.

Two years later I was nearing the end of my degree. The number of classes I took during this time was insane; but the entrepreneur in me, as always, rose to the challenge. This is the point when several of the professors at the university began to suggest, strongly, that I consider a master's degree. Their thinking was, if I were going to start an entrepreneurial consulting business, the new master's of business administration (M.B.A.) in consulting would be invaluable. They were right. Although I knew a lot about entrepreneurship by now I really knew nothing about consulting. However, this was going to add a year and a half to my stay. I thought about it long and hard. I decided that if I was going to do it, I was going to do it right (it didn't hurt that I was sure I could do it in a year). I also thought that if the entrepreneurial consultant venture did not work I would be able to return to the business world much easier with an M.B.A., and it would lend credibility if I ever decided to write a book on entrepreneurship—something I had been thinking about for years. I completed my bachelor of applied arts (B.A.A.) in entrepreneurship in August of 2003 and started my M.B.A. the following week.

In a master's program, you spend a lot of time in front of the classroom presenting. After only one semester, virtually all of my professors started to make, what seemed to me, a strange suggestion. *"Why not become a professor?"* I thought this idea was crazy. I told them, *"I'm not smart enough to be a professor."* The problem was, their argument made sense, **why spend all your time looking for people to help become entrepreneurs when colleges are already full of them?** Additionally, they went on to suggest that many colleges are in desperate need of professors who not only know the academic side of entrepreneurship but the practical side as well. I decided that if I were going even to consider it, I would have to go to a college that offered a Ph.D. in entrepreneurship. It didn't take long to discover that the new problem was that practically no colleges at the time offered such a Ph.D. Most offered a Ph.D. in business with a concentration, typically three to six classes, in entrepreneurship. However, there were six in the world at that time that did offer a Ph.D. in entrepreneurship. One of them was in Louisville, Kentucky. Of course, the next issue was that, although I had a daughter who was grown and in college, I had two younger children too. They were quite young and even though I was divorced I was with them almost every day. I decided that if Louisville accepted me I would still be able to see my kids at least every other weekend. After all, it was only six hours away. Additionally, I decided that if I was able to complete a B.A.A. and an M.B.A. in a total of four years, I should be able to complete a Ph.D. in two or three (I could not have been more wrong, but that is a story for another time). I set out to do everything I could do to get accepted at Louisville. I asked for and received letters of recommendation from everyone who was anyone at CMU. I wrote a letter of intent (an introduction stating why I was a great fit for the program in Louisville). I bought and read books written by all the faculty members in the program and even went so far as to call and set up a meeting with the head of the program—I was accepted.

In August of 2005 I began my Ph.D. at the University of Louisville. This was without question the hardest thing I have ever done. Trust me when I say that anyone who has received a Ph.D. from an accredited university has earned it. It took me three years to complete all the classes and four more years to complete my dissertation (more or less a book on a specific topic for which you become an expert, mine is entrepreneurial mindset). Even though this Ph.D. completely messed up my plan of becoming an entrepreneurial consultant there was one redeeming feature to the scenario. Once you have completed all your coursework and passed both your written and oral exams, you can do your dissertation from just about anywhere in the world. So, once again, the entrepreneur in me came out. Although everyone in the program, and I mean everyone, advised against it I chose to go ABD (All But Dissertation) and to be honest, I would not recommend it either. I accepted a position at Governors State University (GSU) in Illinois. They were looking for someone to create an entrepreneurship program and I was the right man for the job. In addition, they had access to the type of entrepreneurs I needed to do the research for my dissertation. It was a perfect match. Furthermore, they believed in my vision of what was needed to create an entrepreneurship program properly: A program designed not only to expose potential entrepreneurs to the knowledge they needed to know, but one that actually mentored them all the way through the entrepreneurial process if they choose an entrepreneurial path. By the time I completed my dissertation and graduated with a Ph.D. in entrepreneurship from the University of Louisville in May of 2012, I had also created a comprehensive entrepreneurship program at GSU. The program includes a major and a minor in entrepreneurship, designed for people who feel they might want to become an entrepreneur one day. A bachelor of arts in entrepreneurship, designed for those who plan to become entrepreneurs during or immediately following college, and a corporate entrepreneurship specialization under the M.B.A. program for those who are working and understand the importance of becoming corporate entrepreneurs.

Summary of My Qualifications

So to sum it all up, *why is this book the right choice to learn about entrepreneurship?* I have over 20 years of experience as a corporate entrepreneur, 6 years experience as a small business entrepreneur, a bachelor's degree in entrepreneurship, a master of business administration, a doctor of philosophy in entrepreneurship, and have created and implemented an academic program specifically designed for people who want to become entrepreneurs. In short, I am an entrepreneur in every sense of the word—*who better to learn from?*

What This Book Offers

This book is designed with two specific goals in mind. 1) To educate you in the entrepreneurial process and 2) to help you realize that you absolutely can become an entrepreneur, if you so choose. I accomplish these goals by creating a book that focuses specifically on the entrepreneurial process and not small business (yes, there is a significant difference and this will be explained in the book). In addition, I have written this book in a clear and concise manner using examples that make it easy to comprehend the concepts you will be learning. I have also created exercises designed not only to evaluate what you have learned, but also to make you think about how each topic might apply to your own personal journey into entrepreneurship.

In this book, you will learn why entrepreneurship is so important. You will learn what exactly is the difference between a businessperson and an entrepreneur. Ultimately, you will understand what an entrepreneur is and how you can become one. You will learn about the different types of entrepreneurship and the different ways you can be an entrepreneur—there are several. You will also learn how entrepreneurs think differently from others and how you can start to think like an entrepreneur, how to protect yourself from making unethical decisions in your entrepreneurial endeavors, and how you can be emotionally prepared for the inevitable ups and downs of entrepreneurship. You will learn how entrepreneurs locate or create and evaluate entrepreneurial opportunities, and the process you should follow to take advantage of your entrepreneurial opportunity.

What This Book Is Not

This book is designed to give you a solid foundation for truly understanding the entrepreneurial process and what it takes to become an entrepreneur. It is not meant to be all-inclusive. Entrepreneurship is a comprehensive field and no single book can cover everything a person needs to know. This book is intended to be but the first in a series of books designed specifically to guide people who choose to become entrepreneurs down the path to entrepreneurship.

Why the Book Is Written the Way It Is

I am writing this book in what I feel is a unique way, the same way I teach my classes: a cross between a traditional textbook, a how-to book, and an autobiography. I am writing in this manner because I feel it is the best way to ensure that you understand how I know what I am teaching is relevant and accurate. Like most entrepreneurs, I have a problem with just accepting what people tell me (even if it's from experts like me), thus I would be a hypocrite to expect you just to accept what I am telling you as the truth, simply because I have a background in the field. Therefore, throughout this book, where appropriate, I enhance your understanding of certain topics with personal stories and experiences that I hope will help personalize the topics for you. Most experiences are from my life. Others come from the world around us, but all are designed to give you ways to relate the topic personally to your life. Where appropriate, I have added references to the actual research and theories discussed. This is done so you are able to read for yourself the research to help you further understand the entrepreneurial process.

Section 1

Entrepreneurship

In the preface, I suggested that there is far more to entrepreneurship that most people even realize. This is not a reference to the knowledge needed to start a business, but rather the different ways one can go about becoming an entrepreneur, the different types of entrepreneurship that exists, and even the different ways one can remain an entrepreneur throughout their life. Complicating things further is the fact that most people, and even many scholars, cannot even agree on what is and is not entrepreneurship. Therefore, section 1 focuses on specifically what is and is not entrepreneurship. It is important to begin here so we can start with a solid common foundation from which to build. To that end, Chapter 1 focuses on specifically what is and is not entrepreneurship. After this, we explore the need for entrepreneurship in Chapter 2 to help understand just how entrepreneurship affects everyone. In Chapter 3 we look at the difference reasons why one becomes an entrepreneur, in addition to the ways. Culminating in Chapter 4 with a forms entrepreneurship can take including traditional (start-up) entrepreneurship, corporate entrepreneurship, and even a look at social entrepreneurship.

Chapter 1:

What Exactly Is Entrepreneurship

This chapter focuses on what entrepreneurship is and how it differs from other concepts typically associated with traditional business.

Entrepreneurship—Misconceptions

Misconception: Entrepreneurs are Gamblers

One misconception about entrepreneurship is that *entrepreneurs are extreme risk-seekers*, in essence "gamblers." This is one perception we need to dispel right away. **Gamblers** are risk-seekers; they take risk for the mere thrill of it. Although from the perspective of a non-entrepreneur, the risk that an entrepreneur takes may appear to be a form of gambling, research has shown[1] that not only are entrepreneurs primarily not risk-seekers (gamblers), successful entrepreneurs actually tend to be somewhat risk-adverse. This means that, although entrepreneurs are risk-takers, they attempt to avoid all but the most reasonable, or calculated, of risks. Entrepreneurs accomplish such moderation of risk through proper research, careful planning, preparation, and contingencies. In short, the reason entrepreneurs appear to be risk-seeking (gamblers) to some people is a simple case of misinformation; they do not know what the entrepreneur knows.

---

[1] Caliendo, M., Fossen, F., et al. (2009). Risk attitudes of nascent entrepreneurs-new evidence from an experimentally validated survey. *Small Business Economics* 32(2):153 and Keh, H.T., Foo, M.D., et al. (2002). Opportunity evaluation under risky conditions: The cognitive processes of entrepreneurs. *Entrepreneurship Theory and Practice* 27(2): 125.

For example, you see an accident on the side of the road. You stop to see if there is anything you can do to help. As you approach the car, you see a woman dressed in an old worn out sweatshirt and sweatpants, with a pocketknife, just about to stick it in a man's neck. Your first thought might be, *"that is a risky thing to do"* or *"oh my god she could kill him."* However, once you find out that she is actually a surgeon, you realize that there really was not much risk at all. The difference lies in the surgeon's knowledge, training to make such a decision, and skills to perform such an action with minimal risk. The problem with entrepreneurship is that most people do not realize the actual skills and training a good entrepreneur possesses. Additionally, because they often look just like you and me (and sometimes have even less education than we have), we assume they are taking an extreme risk. When in reality, if we knew everything they knew about the topic they are pursuing, we could see that the risk is actually minimal.

Misconception: Starting a Business is Entrepreneurship

Another misconception about entrepreneurship is the belief that entrepreneurship is just the act of starting a business. Entrepreneurship is, at its core, *a way of thinking*. It is a way of thinking that inevitably must lead to some form of action, but starting a business is only one possible entrepreneurial action.

An entrepreneur *can* perform the simple act of starting a business—this is true. However, any businessperson can also perform the exact same action. The difference between what an entrepreneur does in comparison to what a businessperson does lies in the type of business started. Entrepreneurs create entrepreneurial ventures that are unique in some way to all existing businesses. This uniqueness may range from a small but innovative change, such as taking an existing business model and doing something unique with it, to a radical new innovative venture that never existed before. Examples of these would be the idea of putting a previously stand-alone franchise restaurant, in a kiosk form, in a gas station or other such places (**short-term or single-use entrepreneurship**) and the idea of the personal computer (**long-term entrepreneurship**).

The point in both of these examples is that starting the actual business was not a requirement for entrepreneurial behavior to have taken place, nor is being the originator of the concept. **Entrepreneurship** is the creation or location of an opportunity that leads to the creation or location of a means to bring this opportunity to market.[2] Once these two behaviors are complete, the final act of entrepreneurship varies. The entrepreneur could start the business or the entrepreneur could also simply sell the opportunity to a businessperson. Both options are acts of entrepreneurship.

Misconception: Small Business and Entrepreneurship Are the Same

Far too often, entrepreneurship and small business are considered one-and-the-same. This is not the case. **Small business**, quite simply put, is any business that has a small number of employees and minimal yearly sales. Entrepreneurship on the other

---

[2] McGrath, R. G. & MacMillian, I. (2000). *The Entrepreneurial Mindset: Strategies for Continuously Creating Opportunity in an Age of Uncertainty.* Boston: Harvard Business School Press.

hand has nothing to do with size. Entrepreneurship is the manner in which a business is run. Entrepreneurial ventures range in size from a one-person operation making minimal profits to a venture large enough to rival a Fortune 500 company. Once again, the difference lies in the uniqueness of the venture, specifically the product, process, or service, the focus on continuous venture improvement over profit, and the degree to which it is difficult to imitate (inimitable).

Misconception: Once an Entrepreneur, Always an Entrepreneur

Entrepreneurship can be a onetime occurrence. Consequently, some people start out as entrepreneurs and, over time, transition into businesspersons. This occurs when an individual acts in an entrepreneurial manner to start a business and, once the business is formed, typically within 1 to 5 years, adopts **traditional business practices** (i.e., a focus on continuous steady profit growth rather than on continuous venture improvement over profit). This is not to say that all entrepreneurs become businesspersons over time. Some entrepreneurs do in fact remain entrepreneurs. These entrepreneurs continue to be entrepreneurial in practically everything they do throughout their lives. Good examples of these types of individuals are serial and parallel entrepreneurs.

A **serial entrepreneur** is an individual who starts an entrepreneurial venture and once the venture reaches the stage of a traditional business, sells the business and uses the profit to move on to the next entrepreneurial opportunity. **Parallel entrepreneurs** differ from serial entrepreneurs only in the manner in which they handle the transition to a traditional business. Parallel entrepreneurs employ people to run the day-to-day operation of the business and then move on to the next entrepreneurial opportunity. Therefore, while both serial and parallel entrepreneurs continually start new entrepreneurial ventures, serial entrepreneurs typically own but one venture at a time while parallel entrepreneurs tend to own several businesses at any given time with the newest venture typically being the only one that is truly entrepreneurial.

Misconception: Entrepreneurs—Are They Born or Made?

In the late 20th century, one of the biggest debates surrounding entrepreneurship related to whether or not entrepreneurs were self-made or born that way. This is a very good question in general and a very important question for those who are considering entrepreneurship as a career. Prior to the late 20th century, little research relating to entrepreneurship was undertaken. Due to this lack of research on the topic, and because entrepreneurship requires no formal training under law, the majority of people believed that entrepreneurship must be a personal characteristic—much like a natural physical ability or a high IQ.

Let me begin by stating that entrepreneurship is neither a personal characteristic nor a personality trait. Years of academic research,[3] and my own personal experiences, have shown that entrepreneurship is in fact a combination of skill and

---

[3] A tremendous amount of research in the late 20th century was devoted to this topic. Check virtually any academic journal from this period to see this debate. For a good example of this discussion, see Gartner W, (1988), "Who is the entrepreneur? Is the wrong question." *American Journal of Small Business* 12, 4, pp 11-32.

ability. This is important to understand, because if it were in fact a characteristic or a trait, you would have to be born with it. If that were the case, either you already are an entrepreneur or you are not (thus reading this book would be a complete waste of your time).

Many entrepreneurs believe that *entrepreneurial ability* (what they really mean is entrepreneurial mindset), the capacity to locate entrepreneurial opportunities and determine a means to exploit them, is something they were born with. Truthfully, I understand how they might think that way—but they are mistaken. Often, such individuals use the simple argument *"I had no formal entrepreneurial training"* (sometimes even no formal education at all) as the foundation for their claim. What they do not realize is the amount of informal training they have received, more commonly referred to as trial and error or even trial-by-fire. These entrepreneurs most certainly have received entrepreneurial training. They have learned by trying and failing repeatedly until they figured out how to do it successfully. What they possess that you may not currently possess is a strong reason or motivator to keep trying when traditional employment is an easier or safer option to follow.

Another argument used to support the claim that entrepreneurs are born that way is personality type. Such individuals point to a seemingly inherent ability to talk to just about anyone, the ability to look fear in the face and to push right past it, the confidence to try almost anything no matter the consequences, and even a mystical ability to see opportunities where others cannot no matter how hard they try. Again, I would have to say they are mistaken. I agree that individuals who already possess such abilities likely find entrepreneurship inherently easier to pursue than those not currently possessing such personal attributes do. However, all of these attributes are learnable, or if you choose not to learn them, you can always hire or collaborate with people who possess these abilities. Contrary to popular opinion, entrepreneurship does not have to be a one-person show.

The important thing when talking to such people is not to buy into this line of thought. Based on training and experience, it is my belief that such claims are little more than a means to explain why such individuals do not know how to teach entrepreneurship, or as an excuse for them not becoming entrepreneurs themselves. I can assure you that I have taught many people how to become entrepreneurs who did not have the personality traits or characteristics commonly associated with so-called "natural" entrepreneurs, and most importantly, I did not teach them how to start a business, any business professor can do that. I taught them how to think, and act, like an entrepreneur, in short, how to create an entrepreneurial mindset within themselves.

At this point, I hope you are beginning to understand that virtually everyone is capable of becoming an entrepreneur—the only real requirement is the willingness to work hard and the commitment to learn how. Now we can move on to discussing what exactly entrepreneurship is and is not.

★★★★★★★★★★

Let me assure you I was not born an entrepreneur. Growing up, I was a very shy child. I withdrew from interacting with people and terrified at the mere thought of having to interact with people I did not know. In fact, even to this day the thought of talking to anyone, let alone a large crowd, about a topic I am not familiar with scares me to death. Nevertheless, ask me to speak to anyone about a topic I know, such as entrepreneurship, and I become the world's biggest evangelist—eager to get in front of any size crowd to share what I know and what I have learned.

★★★★★★★★★★

Entrepreneurship—the Intersection of Entrepreneur and Opportunity

Entrepreneurship occurs at the nexus between an individual and an opportunity.[4] What this means is that entrepreneurship only happens when the right person (someone with an entrepreneurial mindset—who is motivated to act) meets the right opportunity (a truly unique concept). Before we take a closer look at this statement, it is first necessary to understand each of these three elements individually.

Entrepreneurial Mindset

An **entrepreneurial mindset** is the way of thinking that allows a person to locate, or create, entrepreneurial opportunities and determine the best possible means of exploiting such opportunities[5] (remember exploitation is not a bad thing unless you make it so).

---

[4] Shane, S. A. (2003). *A General Theory of Entrepreneurship: The Individual-Opportunity Nexus.* Northampton, MA: Edward Elgar Publishing.
[5] McGrath, R.G. & MacMillan, I. (2000), *The Entrepreneurial Mindset: Strategies for Continuously Creating Opportunity in an Age of Uncertainty.* Boston: Harvard Business School Press.

Entrepreneurial Mindset

Motivation to Action

Entrepreneurship Takes Place

Opportunity

Think of an entrepreneurial mindset as the lens through which the entrepreneur views the world. This mindset allows an entrepreneur to see obstructions not as problems but as opportunities to solve a problem. Where others see roadblocks, entrepreneurs see the opportunity to build a new road. Where others see tragedy, entrepreneurs see opportunities to prevent such tragedies from occurring to others. Where others see limitations in life, entrepreneurs see opportunities to overcome. Therefore, the first component necessary for entrepreneurship to occur is the existence of an entrepreneurial mindset.

Unfortunately, the ability to locate or create entrepreneurial opportunities and determine a viable means of exploitation, on its own, is not enough for entrepreneurship to occur. Without the opportunity and the motivation to act, potential opportunities remain unseen or ignored by the individual. In support of this statement, all you have to do is ask yourself how many times you have seen a new product, process, or service and you, or someone you know, said, "Hey—I thought of that a long time ago." Often times a new idea may not actually be that new. Sometimes what is new is that someone finally did something about it.

Motivation to Action

Entrepreneurs are motivated. Motivation can take many forms. Some entrepreneurs are motivated by a need for independence (to be their own boss). Others are motivated by a need to increase their emotional self-worth. Still others are motivated by a need to overcome some disadvantage (lack of education, unemployment, social standing, disability [learning, mental, or physical], etc.). The reality is anything that is capable of compelling a person to take action (good or bad) is a potential motivator for entrepreneurship.

Opportunity

In my experience, when it comes to opportunities most people walk through life with blinders on. The comment I hear the most from people who want to become an entrepreneur for the first time is, *"I would become an entrepreneur in a second, if I could just find an opportunity."* Opportunities are everywhere. Not all of these are entrepreneurial opportunities, but good opportunities are everywhere. Each of us walk right past loads of opportunities every day, and even worse, we ignore even more opportunities that are virtually handed to us by friends, family, coworkers, and even total strangers (but I will go into greater detail about this in a later chapter). The problem is that most people do not possess the mindset needed to recognize these opportunities, or if they do, they are not able to determine a real means of exploiting the opportunity. This is what makes entrepreneurs so different. Entrepreneurs are able to see, or truly listen for, opportunities in their everyday lives. When they find one, they are capable of determining the best possible way of exploiting the opportunity and quickly evaluating its potential. They can do this because they have developed this entrepreneurial mindset.

The interaction between entrepreneur and opportunity is the spark that ignites the entrepreneurial flame. Much like a fire cannot exist without three basic elements (oxygen, fuel, and heat) all coming together in the right combination; entrepreneurship cannot exist without three essentials also coming together. These prerequisites for entrepreneurship are a person with an entrepreneurial mindset, the motivation to act, and an opportunity. For example, if an individual possesses an entrepreneurial mindset and the motivation to act, but has not located an opportunity, they will begin the search for an opportunity. This search is in fact entrepreneurial behavior; however, such behavior in and of itself is not entrepreneurship.

Entrepreneurship will not occur until an opportunity has been located and a means of exploiting it has been determined and action taken.

On the other hand, if an individual possesses an entrepreneurial mindset, and has located an opportunity, this is also not enough for entrepreneurship to take place. What is obviously missing is the motivation to act. If this individual does not have a reason to act on the created or located opportunity, the opportunity is lost because they have no reason to take action. Motivation can come in many forms, the loss of a job, the need to be in charge, or any such situation that acts as a motivator. However, without the motivation to act entrepreneurship will again not occur.

The most misunderstood situation is when a person possesses the motivation to act, and has located an opportunity, but does not have an entrepreneurial mindset. In this situation, what occurs is often mistaken for entrepreneurship. This is because although an individual with the motivation to act may seek out an opportunity, if they lack an entrepreneurial mindset, they will at best locate existing business opportunities. The existence of such an entrepreneurial mindset allows individuals to locate more than existing business opportunities, it allows them the ability to create or locate entrepreneurial opportunities. This is a key aspect of the entrepreneurial process because business opportunities only offer owners' average returns on their investment of time and money; whereas entrepreneurial opportunities afford an individual the potential for extended, above the average, return on investment.

As you can see, only the unique combination of an entrepreneur mindset, the motivation to act, and the location of an entrepreneurial opportunity truly afford an individual the real possibility of entrepreneurship.

Summary

Entrepreneurship is much more than people think. At its core, entrepreneurship is a mindset (way of thinking) that allows an individual to locate or create entrepreneurial opportunities. This mindset also affords the individual the ability and the motivation to determine means bring these opportunities to market for a profit (exploitation). Through this knowledge, the complexity of answering a question like, "What exactly is entrepreneurship?," is revealed. Although this chapter has addressed many of the misconceptions surrounding entrepreneurship, and explained much of what entrepreneurship is, a great deal remains in regards to the process of becoming an entrepreneur. In the chapters to follow these topics will be addressed in detail.

Chapter 2:

The Need for Entrepreneurship

In this chapter the primary focus will be on the importance of entrepreneurship; basically, why do we need it? It is necessary to explore this need in order to show how entrepreneurship has real value, not just for those who choose to become entrepreneurs, but also for all of us.

The Entrepreneur: An Agent for Change

If you really think about it, we have entrepreneurs to thank for pretty much everything that we have today. Without the influence of entrepreneurs, most of us would still be living in caves, naked, and walking everywhere (and did I mention computers or cell phones?). Now you might say that is crazy, entrepreneurs are not the only ones who create things, inventors do too, and you would be right. The problem is that, strictly speaking, inventors invent and most of the time that is where it ends. Sure, inventors often create to fulfill personal needs, and may even provide those around them with the benefits of their inventions. However, this is usually where it ends. The reason is simple. The driving force for a true inventor is creation. Inventors enjoy the thrill of creating something that did not previously exist. Once they have created something, they often move on to the next new and exciting creation. Often these creations have no real world importance or value and when they do, most inventors are scared off once they realize they have no idea how or what it will take to turn their invention into a marketable product or service. This is where entrepreneurs come in.

Entrepreneurs, again strictly speaking, find unique ideas known as **entrepreneurial opportunities** and locate or create a means of exploiting these ideas. Before we go any further, we need to pause for a moment and talk about the word *exploit*. All too often words like exploit are seen only in the negative context. In the case of entrepreneurship, the word **exploit** simply means to develop a way to bring a product or service to market for a profit. In this context exploit does not mean to take advantage of someone. Entrepreneurs are not conmen. True entrepreneurs are, simply put, people who find ways to make things happen. Think of entrepreneurs, for now, as facilitators. The driving force behind the entrepreneur is problem solving. Satisfaction for the entrepreneur thus comes from solving the problem of getting the inventor's idea to market. However, this is not the end of the process. Once entrepreneurs determine a means of exploiting an opportunity they then convey that means to others, typically businesspersons.

Businesspersons are those engaged in providing products or services to the commercial or industrial markets. The driving force behind the businessperson is profit. Satisfaction, for the businessperson, derives from finding an economic means of producing or supplying a product or service and selling it for the highest price the market will accept, thus maximizing profits. If we think of these three players (the inventor, the entrepreneur, and the businessperson) as a chain in the process of providing new products and services to the market, we can see how the statement that entrepreneurs represent the driving force behind virtually all that we have holds true.

Inventor   **Entrepreneur**   **Businessperson**

Chapter 2: The Need for Entrepreneurship

This is a very simple version of the process and many variations of how a new product finds its way to market do occur. There are inventors/entrepreneurs, and entrepreneur/businesspersons, and even inventor/entrepreneur/businesspersons. The key is, without the entrepreneur, the chain is broken and practically nothing that is invented would find its way to the market. In fact, the market might not even exist if it were not for the entrepreneur. Thus, the entrepreneur is, in essence, the agent for change in the process of bringing virtually all new products and services to the business environment.

Entrepreneurship and the Business Environment

Because the primary purpose of entrepreneurship is to bridge the gap between invention and business, entrepreneurship has a direct effect on business environments in several ways.

Economic Growth

The amount of entrepreneurial activity is directly related to a country's economy. Research suggests that when an economy is stagnant, or in decline, entrepreneurial activity increases dramatically.[1] This occurs because in such an environment people often find themselves with limited possibilities for growth (stuck in a dead end job) or even worse unemployed.

---

[1] Acs, Z. (2006). How is entrepreneurship good for economic growth? *Innovations* Winter: 97-107.

In general, people are not satisfied with mere survival. We aspire to be more than our current circumstances. In essence, we want to be all that we can be. We want our friends and family to be proud of us for what we've accomplished, and when we feel that the means to excel in our lives are limited, we look for alternatives. When placed in situations of limitation or constraint, such as unemployment or the inability to increase our current income, we tend to look for alternate means. In normal economic times, the majority of people who find themselves in this situation will simply look for new employment (approximately 94%), one that offers the ability to improve our economic situation. The other 6% look for entrepreneurial opportunities.[2] However, when times are hard this can change.

When countries have extreme unemployment rates such as Haiti (70% in 2000), and no social welfare systems, individuals have little choice but to become entrepreneurs or perish. Although under these extreme conditions some individuals will resort to illegal entrepreneurship (i.e., fraud, the sale of illegal substances or services, etc.), most seek out legal means of entrepreneurship. For example, in India where nearly 30% of the country's population lives below the poverty level, entrepreneurs have created recycling systems capable of reclaiming up to 80% of waste (compared to 32.5% in the United States). Although these "Slumdog"

---

[2] Fairle, R.W. (2012). *Kauffman Index of Entrepreneurial Activity*, March.

Chapter 2: The Need for Entrepreneurship

entrepreneurs are not getting rich, they have created a unique means of improving their personal situation. From this example, we can see that when environmental circumstances limit an individual's possibility for growth, those possessing an *entrepreneurial mindset* (an entrepreneurial way of thinking) begin to look for unique ways to improve their situation by means of entrepreneurial opportunities.

Although entrepreneurship occurs in both good times and bad, in times of economic hardship more individuals turn to entrepreneurship out of necessity. Consequently, we can state that entrepreneurship acts as a means of stimulating economic growth in good times, and even more so in bad times. This is why entrepreneurship is a prerequisite for true economic growth.[3] For this reason, a country's economic growth is often dependent on the degree to which it encourages and supports entrepreneurship.

Employment Growth

Another way entrepreneurship affects the business environment is through the creation of new jobs. Some entrepreneurs create new businesses, and many new businesses in turn create jobs. Thus, entrepreneurship fundamentally creates new jobs as a side effect of the process. Research has shown that perhaps as much as 90% of all new jobs are a direct result of entrepreneurship.[4] More importantly, entrepreneurs work hard to keep their workforce once they have it. It's been said that entrepreneurial ventures are the engine of true employment creation,[5] so let's take a deeper look into these claims.

---

[3] Thurik, R. (2008). *The World Entrepreneurship Forum*.
[4] Henrekson, M., & Johansson, D. (2010). Gazelles as job creators: A survey and interpretation of the evidence. *Small Business Economics* 35(2): 227-244.
[5] Erken, H., Donselaar, P., & Thurik, R. (2008). Total factor productivity and the role of entrepreneurship. *Jena Economic Research Papers* #2008-019, Jena: Friedrich Schiller University and Max Planck Institute of Economics. & Fritsch, M. (2008). How does new business formation affect regional development? Introduction to the special issue. *Small Business Economics* 30: 1-14.

Employee-Employer Loyalty

In general, the goal of business is to create value for its **stakeholders**, a person, group, or organization that has an interest in the business. One of the greatest means of creating stakeholder value is efficiency. As companies become more efficient at what they do, they often find they no longer need as many people to get the same amount of output. In general, when this occurs one of two things will happen, the company finds a way to sell more product (or services) or they reduce the workforce. Far too often, it is the latter. Thus, in industrial economies unskilled **human capital**, (employees) are frequently considered expendable. Entrepreneurs tend to think differently.

Entrepreneurial ventures typically start small. This means that entrepreneurs are likely to spend more time working with and alongside their employees. Such closeness tends to create a greater personal bond with employees than is typically found in most existing businesses. Additionally, the newness of a venture often makes it difficult to hire good employees (many potential employees see the uncertainty of an entrepreneurial venture as just too much of a risk). It is for these reasons that most entrepreneurs work very hard not to reduce their workforce. When entrepreneurs become more efficient at producing their product or providing their service, or sales drop, they tend to work hard to locate new markets to keep their existing employees working rather than cutting back on the total number of employees. This resistance to reducing the workforce suggests that entrepreneurs see the loss of human capital (employees) as a situation to avoid at all cost. It is important to understand that although loyalty within entrepreneurial ventures may tend to be high, this does not equate to job security. If the venture fails, jobs will be lost. However, the tendency to create new jobs, coupled with a propensity toward employer-employee loyalty (and of course a healthy drive to succeed), lead to an environment where the continuous search for new opportunities (an entrepreneurial economy), not higher profit margins (an industrial economy), is the norm.

In whole, in a business environment where entrepreneurship is supported and strongly encouraged, an entrepreneurial economy should emerge that creates a greater number of jobs, and higher wages[6] due to the continuous focus on entrepreneurial opportunities, rather than production efficiency.

Entrepreneurship and the Economy

To begin, it is important to understand there are several different types of economies. For our purposes, economies are defined by the primary means of financial support for the majority of the population in a region (how do most people make a living). Thus, an agricultural economy exists when the majority of the gross

---

[6] Acs, Z.J., Fitzroy, F.R., & Smith, I. (2002). High-technology employment and R&D in cities: heterogeneity vs specialization. *Annals of Regional Science* 36(3): 373-386; Scarpetta, S., Hemmings, P., Tressel, T., & Woo, J. (2002). *The role of policy and institutions for productivity and firm dynamics: evidence from micro and industry data*, OECD Economics Department Working Paper 329. Paris: OECD.

income from a region is the result of farming crops and raising livestock. The two economies we will be discussing are industrial and entrepreneurial economies as they relate to the creation of new products and services (i.e., innovation).

Industrial economies thrive on uniformity, stability, and mass production. In such economic conditions, businesses focus on economies of scale and conservation of resources, as mentioned earlier, maximizing profit. Within such an environment, the process of innovation is, for all intents and purposes, closed. With organizations focusing on making long runs of standardized products, innovation is typically limited to the introduction of small product improvements with predictable regularity. Because this type of economy revolves around stability, specialization, certainty, and predictability, in essence *continuity*, they tend to excel at incremental innovation.

Incremental innovations are a series of small improvements to an existing product intended to maintain or improve a company's competitive advantage over its competition. Most noticeable in high-tech industries, such as computers and cell phones, this form of innovation seldom leads to revolutionary or game changing advancements. The focus on incremental innovation, although essential to the success of an industrial economy, can often leave companies blind to radical innovations that will threaten the current market.

★★★★★★★★★★

The Eastman Kodak Company dominated the photographic film industry in the United States for over 100 years. In 1976, 90% of all photographic film sold in the United States came from Kodak. However, in January 2012 Kodak had to file Chapter 11 bankruptcy for protection against its creditors. It was in real financial trouble. Why—people stopped buying film and turned to digital cameras. So why did Kodak not see this coming? After all, they developed the digital camera in 1975. Executives at Kodak could not grasp the idea that people could be happy with digital photos. At the time, their thinking might have made sense from a shortsighted perspective. The technology did not exist to print film-quality pictures from a digital camera. Storage of digital pictures was expensive, a 30-megabyte hard drive in 1990 cost $450. Moreover, when sales of film began to drop off in 2001, executives attributed the loss not to the sale of digital cameras by its competitors, but to the September 11th attacks on the World Trade Center in New York City. In essence, the focus on incremental improvement (better quality film pictures at a lower price) caused Kodak to miss the bigger picture—things change.

What Kodak did not see, due to their focus on incremental improvement, were companies in 1991 such as Iris Graphics (with their model 3047) that were beginning to manufacture photo-quality printers. Although the first models were hard to maintain and expensive ($126,000), the new printers were making it possible to match film-quality pictures. Companies like Iris, with a focus on incremental improvement, continually improved the ease of use and reduced the cost of photo-quality printers. In 2013 such printers were available for as low as $199 (Epson Artisan 1430). At the same time, manufacturers of hard drive technology were also focused on incremental improvements, making storage capacity increase and price decrease (by 2013 the price of a 1-terabyte hard drive dropped to $80, approximately 80% less cost with more than 30,000 times the amount of storage from 1990).

What Kodak missed with their focus on incremental innovation was that others were creating innovations in their own markets that would eventually render the photographic film obsolete. Even worse, they themselves had created the core technology that had made it possible, and had failed to see its true potential, setting the stage for their own financial difficulties nearly 35 years later. This is not an isolated incident. Similar stories exist with many of the Fortune 500 companies of the 20th century including IBM, Xerox, and many more. What they all have in common is the singular focus on incremental innovation with the failure to notice radical innovations that would change the marketplace forever.

★★★★★★★★★★

Entrepreneurial economies do not adhere to traditional business or leadership roles. Entrepreneurial economies embrace newness and uncertainty, focusing on exploration, innovation, and exploitation. Within this type of environment, the innovation process is very much open. Such an economy revolves around creativity,

Chapter 2: The Need for Entrepreneurship

communication, knowledge, and intelligence; in essence, *change,* and due to this focus, tends to excel at radical innovation.

Radical innovations are original concepts that change customer expectations. In addition radical innovations, also known as breakthrough and disruptive innovation (sometimes even market killer), often replace existing products, services, and processes by significantly changing consumers' expectations of an existing product, service, or process. Such radical innovations are, for all intents and purposes, game changers. Examples of radical innovation are indoor plumbing, electricity, the telegraph, railroads, refrigeration, the automobile, the airplane, television, personal computers, cable television, the internet, and cell phones, just to name a few. Radical innovations change our lives. They permanently raise the bar for what we expect from a product, service, or process. This form of innovation is an essential component to an entrepreneurial economy. Without radical innovation, entrepreneurial economies would not exist.

Entrepreneurial economies are often born of social systems where individual creativity, problem solving, and critical thinking are prized over conformity and complacency—**entrepreneurial societies**. Such societies exist when the individual, or groups of individuals, are encouraged to try new things. Where failure is not only tolerated but also encouraged (I will talk more about his concept later in this book). One in which effort is rewarded over accomplishment. Don't get me wrong, not everyone in such an economy will be an entrepreneur. Just as entrepreneurs exist within industrial economies, non-entrepreneurs must also exist within the entrepreneurial economy. If they did not, who would build the product or provide the service until such entrepreneurial ventures grew to maturity and became traditional businesses capable of providing their product, service, or process to the masses? The difference is choice. Acting and thinking differently, in an entrepreneurial economy, is the norm—never looked down upon. Asking questions is encouraged and challenging the status quo is expected. In such a society, although not everyone will be an entrepreneur, anyone can be if they so choose.

Both entrepreneurial and industrial economies are necessary for a truly balanced global economy. Each has its own strengths which act to complement the other's weaknesses. In an ideal global economy, regions with large populations and limited resources can focus on industrialization and efficiency of production. Regions with vast amounts of natural resources can focus on providing and maintaining renewable materials, and regions with small populations and limited resources can focus on research and the dissemination of knowledge. The key is that in all regions radical innovation is encouraged and fostered through the support of individual creativity, problem solving, and critical thinking. In such an ideal global economy, individuals would be encouraged to move to the area that is best suited to who they are, or who they want to be, rather than expected to remain in the region of their birth. Furthermore, in an ideal global economy, young adults would be encouraged, if not required, to spend time working and living in each of these regions so they are truly informed before they make a decision on what area is best suited for them. Such a system would be similar to what college students are doing now, by taking an assortment of classes before making a career choice.

Summary

As you can see, entrepreneurship is important to our everyday lives. Without it, most of the luxuries we enjoy, and the ones we can look forward to, would not exist.

Remember, inventors create and businesspeople supply, but only entrepreneurship brings these two together.

★★★★★★★★★★

In this chapter, the difficulties an entrepreneur faces when hiring for a new entrepreneurial venture were discussed. To expand on this issue, the following personal experience.

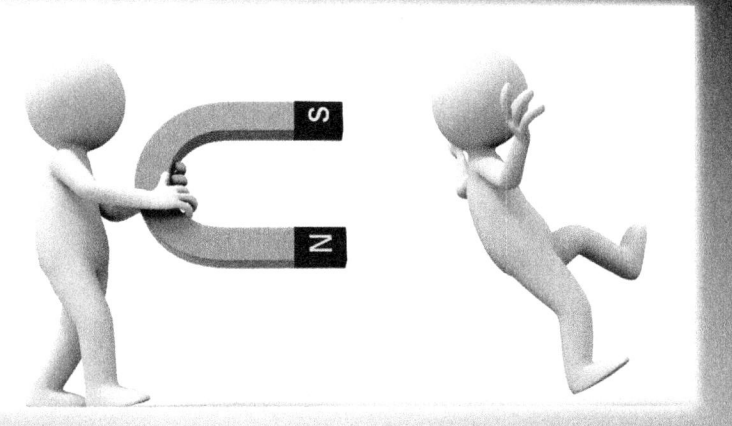

When I started my first company, I was surprised to learn that hiring good people was extremely difficult. I found that even my family and friends were unwilling to take the risk. When I was able to locate people who were willing to take a chance on a budding new venture, most people felt it necessary to take a leave from their current job (so they could go back if it didn't work) or only worked with me as a second or part-time job. When you think of it, can you blame them? Although I was willing to pay them more than they were currently making, I could offer no health insurance, and more importantly no guarantee that the company would make it. Now if you are young and have no responsibilities, or if you are already unemployed, you might be willing to take the chance; however, most people have families to support. This often means that no matter how much they might like to take the chance on you and your new venture, or no matter how much money you offer, people often just cannot afford to take the risk. Once you learn this as a **entrepreneur**, a person in the early stages of entrepreneurship, you realize that finding good people who can and will take a chance on you and your business is almost as hard as finding the money to get started.

Chapter 2: The Need for Entrepreneurship 31

As far as hiring people other than family and friends, well, when you start in your basement working 16 to 18 hours a day, you tend to be quite hesitant about hiring people you do not know (or at least you should be). Once the business grew to the point that it could sustain the cost of its own space, the trouble was not over. While there were plenty of people unemployed at the time, I found that a surprising number of these people were unemployed for good reason. Now I am not going to go into detail, but I typically had to hire and then let go (or they quit) as many as four people in order to find one person who was capable and willing to work in my entrepreneurial venture and, based on my discussions with other entrepreneurs, this is quite common.

★★★★★★★★★★

So why am I sharing this story with you? It is important to understand the difficulties in hiring people when you are a nascent entrepreneur. When it is this difficult to find good people who are capable and willing to take a chance on an entrepreneurial venture, a strong bond exists; you care about your people on a personal level and they care about you. This is why entrepreneurs tend to do whatever it takes to keep their people working.

★★★★★★★★★★

Chapter 3:

The Equifinal Nature of Entrepreneurship

For this chapter our focus will be on the equifinal nature of entrepreneurship. In short, the reality that a person can take many different paths, all of which can lead to the same destination—entrepreneurship.

"If you don't know where you're going, any road will get you there, so why not choose the one that is right for you?

Entrepreneurial Pathways

An **intention** is a plan to act in a specific manner, toward a given phenomenon, at a particular place and time.[1] Without the presence of the four components of *action*, *object*, *place,* and *time*, a fully formed intention does not exist. Due to the equifinal nature of entrepreneurship, we can use the strength of these four components as a means of determining the likely path a person might take to entrepreneurship.

No Entrepreneurial Intentions

Individuals with no entrepreneurial intention are those who have no *plan* to become an entrepreneur (*object*) and thus have formed no intentions as to when (*time*) and where (*place*) they might begin to take on entrepreneurial behavior. Essentially, all four of the essential components for the formation of entrepreneurial intentions are missing. Initially you might think that someone with no entrepreneurial intentions would never become an entrepreneur—end of story. It is easy to understand this perception. Why would anyone who obviously did not want to, decide to become an

---

[1] Fishbein, M., & Ajzen, I. (2009). <u>Predicting and Changing Behavior: A Reasoned Action Approach.</u> New York: Taylor & Francis, Inc.

entrepreneur?

Sometimes, in fact more often than you might think, people find themselves in circumstances where traditional employment is not an option. It is therefore out of necessity that some individuals will choose to become entrepreneurs. After all, if you cannot get work and you do not live in a society that offers you unemployment or welfare, what other choice do you have? You have to survive, and the only alternative may be to do something illegal, or create a means of supporting yourself—entrepreneurship. Your first thought might be, "But I don't have to worry, I do live in a society that helps those who are unable to find work." Yes, but that is not the only way that individuals can be, in a way, forced into entrepreneurship. If we turn to the academic literature, we find that individuals who feel they are at a disadvantage when it comes to the job market also tend to consider entrepreneurship as a viable means of increasing their current social and economic status. This **disadvantage theory**[2] suggests that individuals may choose entrepreneurship solely as a reaction to real or perceived barriers in the labor market. Because these individuals feel handicapped due to age, low education, lack of language proficiency, learning, mental, or physical disabilities, minority status, immigration status, sexual orientation, or any circumstance that they perceive as limiting their ability to succeed, they will seek alternatives to traditional employment as a survival mechanism. One of the best ways to accomplish this is entrepreneurship.

Another reason individuals with no entrepreneurial intention may choose to become entrepreneurs is as a means of correcting a previous life choice. For example, immigrates, prostitutes, drug dealers, and other such individuals often work illegally

---

[2] Light, I. (1979). Disadvantaged minorities in self-employment. *International Journal of Comparative Sociology* 36: 968-981.; Mora, M. T., & Davila, A. (2005). Ethnic group size, linguistic isolation, and immigrant entrepreneurship in the USA. *Entrepreneurship and Regional Development* 17(5): 389.; Willsdon, J. (2005). Homosexual entrepreneurs: Different but the same. *Irish Journal of Management* 26(1): 107.

(often as illegal entrepreneurs) simply as a perceived means of survival. Given the opportunity, I believe that most, if not all, would choose to become legal entrepreneurs. Individuals with felonies also often find their choices of employment seriously limited even after paying their debt to society. In these situations, such individuals would also likely consider entrepreneurship as a way to alter, or improve their current social and economic standing.

One final way that entrepreneurship can occur, without prior entrepreneurial intentions, are situations where individuals happen or stumble across an opportunity. In these situations, an individual with no intention of, or urge to, become an entrepreneur comes across an incredible opportunity. One so good it is just not possible for them to pass it up. In these types of situations, they may take advantage of the opportunity and realize that they like entrepreneurship and continue, or they sell the opportunity as early as possible and return to their former employment.

Low Entrepreneurial Intentions

Individuals with low entrepreneurial intentions are typically persons who want to be, or are not ruling out the option of becoming, an entrepreneur one day. Thus, the *object* component exists. These individuals, however, are in no hurry or rush to become entrepreneurs. Consequently, the *action, place,* and *time* components are missing. This lack of three of the components needed for the formation of entrepreneurial intentions does not mean that entrepreneurship will never take place. What it means is that until the individuals feel they are ready, no effort will be made to determine what type of entrepreneurial behavior they may undertake (*action*) at a specific *place* and *time*.

A good example of someone with low entrepreneurial intention is a person who wants to become an entrepreneur, but has just graduated high school or college. They are often young, want to start a family, get a home, and just settle into a traditional life for now. They often need to purchase a reliable car and other such necessities in order to begin their new life on their own. If they went to college, they often have a great deal of student loans to repay. Because of these pressing needs, such individuals will typically put their dream of becoming an entrepreneur on hold. At this stage in their life, they are more comfortable entering into the traditional work environment as a safe means of satisfying their personal needs, and getting their life under control. Once they become established and feel they have security, often as they are nearing retirement age, only then will they typically feel comfortable enough to pursue their entrepreneurial passion. It is at this point such individuals will begin to determine when, where, and how (*time, place,* and *action*) they are going to become an entrepreneur.

Moderate Entrepreneurial Intentions

People with moderate entrepreneurial intentions are, in a sense, the opposite of those with low entrepreneurial intentions. They want to become an entrepreneur (*object*) right away (*time*). However, they are not sure what they are going to do or how they are going to do it (*action* and *place*). Rather than jumping into entrepreneurship they wait until they find or locate an entrepreneurial opportunity. Because they are not ready to undertake a specific form of entrepreneur behavior, they instead enter the traditional job market. Yet, the entire time they are working for others they are searching for or trying to create a good entrepreneurial opportunity.

Such individuals are eager and willing to undertake entrepreneurship. They just need to find or create the right opportunity to do so. Often entrepreneurial ideas come from experience. Therefore, this process makes perfect sense for younger people, those who simply do not possess enough experiences to draw from in order to locate or create an opportunity. In essence, such individuals are using their work experiences as a means of gathering the first hand knowledge needed to spark the creative process leading to the location or creation of an entrepreneurial opportunity.

At this point, it is important to talk about entrepreneurial opportunities for a moment. One of the first questions I get from people who fall into this group, once they find out I am an entrepreneur and a professor of entrepreneurship, is, "What kind of business should I start?" Unfortunately, the answer is never what they want to hear. However, the answer is simple, I cannot tell you what business is best for you—*no one can*. In fact, if someone tries to tell you the perfect business to be in—**RUN**.

Either they are trying to sell you something or they just do not understand what entrepreneurship really is. No one can tell you the best entrepreneurial opportunity to pursue. Why? The reason is simple, the moment a person begins telling everyone competition exists. Let me explain, if I write a book, sell DVDs, and hold seminars on the newest entrepreneurial opportunity, the moment I begin doing so (no matter how great the opportunity might have been) the opportunity is doomed to, at best, mediocrity and, at worst, certain failure. The reason is if I am successful I am not just telling you, I am telling thousands if not millions of other people too.

★★★★★★★★★★

    In the early 1980s I was a young man fresh out of high school. I borrowed the money from my parents for a down payment and bought an old house that needed a lot of work for almost nothing (actually, it should have been condemned). I started fixing it up every night after work. After two years of living in a construction zone, and working every night after work until I almost dropped, I finally finished fixing up the house. I then immediately put the house up for sale and ultimately sold it for double what I had put into it. Just to give you an idea of how much money I made, I made the same amount of money from the sale of the house as I did working my job that year.

    I took the money I had earned from the sale and bought another fixer upper and began the process all over again. At the time, it was easy to make money this way. Few people knew about this opportunity and profitable houses were easy to find. If this sounds familiar, it should. In the mid 1980s the housing market crashed when interest rates went through the roof, and people just stopped buying houses. For this reason, several real estate people and flippers (people doing what I was doing) started writing books, selling DVDs, and holding seminars on "how to get rich in real estate" and "how to buy with no money down." After millions of people bought the books and DVDs, and attended the seminars, they started buying up old houses like they were going out of style. This drove up the price of the old fixer uppers to the point you could not make any real money flipping them. See, what you need to know is, if everyone knows about an opportunity there is no longer any real money to be made in it due to competition.

    Today it is even worse, there are several television shows about people flipping houses. The problem is, they never show you or tell you about the thousands of people who lose everything trying. This is because most houses, like the ones I described, are now only in areas where no one wants to live. They learned the hard way that no matter how beautiful you make the house, if it is in an area that people are not willing to, or are afraid to, live in, people are just not going to buy it. Therefore, when someone tries to sell you something geared toward teaching the right business to get into, ask yourself this, "If it is such a great opportunity why are you telling everyone?" I bet, if you could read their mind, the real answer would be, "I can't make money at it anymore so I figure I can make money off of telling you how to do it. I don't care if you lose your shirt doing it, as long as I get paid." In addition, just so you know, free seminars are not free; they are designed to get you excited so you will buy their books and DVDs. Just go by the motto I use and you should be fine. If it sounds too good to be true, it probably is—pass on it.

★★★★★★★★★★

Strong Entrepreneurial Intentions

Individuals with strong entrepreneurial intention are those who are choosing to pursue entrepreneurship (*object*) as a career. For these individuals, intention formation is fully underway. Such individuals are actively searching for an entrepreneurial opportunity (*action*) to act upon, while at the same time seeking out and acquiring the knowledge and training needed to act immediately (*place* and *time*) once the opportunity has been located or created.

Before we discuss this concept further, it is necessary to take a moment and talk about the opinions of many existing entrepreneurs. The consensus of some very successful entrepreneurs has been that entrepreneurship is not something that can be taught, it must be lived. With the greatest respect to these entrepreneurs, I have to say,

"You are wrong." It is understandable why these entrepreneurs might think this way; they believe they had no training. The reality is they absolutely were taught how to be entrepreneurs, they just did not learn in a traditional academic environment. When these entrepreneurs began their entrepreneurial training there were no academics or schools to teach them. They had to teach themselves, and they did—the hard way. They learned by trying and failing repeatedly. Each time picking themselves up, learning from their failures, and trying again until they eventually learned what they needed to know to become successful entrepreneurs, and for this, we must thank them because it is by studying these entrepreneurs we have learned what you need to know in order to improve your chances for success.

Luckily, this form of learning (i.e., the hard way) is no longer necessary. Years of academic research have now yielded much of the knowledge and skills necessary to train individuals how to become entrepreneurs without having to go through the "School of Hard Knocks." Just as is the case with any profession, an entrepreneurial education cannot guarantee success. However, such an education does afford individuals the knowledge they need. It also affords them the opportunity to test out their ideas and potential business concepts in a safe, structured, and mentored environment, thus increasing their chances of early success.

In my experience, it is younger people who tend to possess strong entrepreneurial intention. Such individuals tend to be students in high school who are considering a career in entrepreneurship. We are talking about people new to the job market who are disgruntled with their prospects for advancement and those who find themselves downsized (unemployed). Many of these individuals see entrepreneurship as an excellent means of taking control of their future. Now this does not mean that everyone with strong entrepreneurial intentions is going to go to college, many will still choose the hard way to learn the entrepreneurial process. However, this is because the education system for entrepreneurship is really rather new. Only since the early 1980s has academia really begun to offer courses of any real consequence in relation to entrepreneurial training.

> ★ ★ ★ ★ ★ ★ ★ ★ ★ ★
>
> This is for those who still may be skeptical of the idea that entrepreneurship can be taught. At one time or another, the same was likely said about every profession. Not that many years ago there was no such thing as a surgeon. Dentists of this era were often called upon to operate on people. Although the success rate was dismal, people had few alternatives. How did these people learn to be surgeons? Unfortunately for their patients, they learned through trial and error (sound familiar?). Therefore, the argument that entrepreneurship cannot be taught is invalidated by the simple fact that at one time, every profession started as a somewhat mystical gift, with a high failure rate, which only a few people could do because they were born with the gift. Are we still perfecting the methodology? Yes, but the reality is we now know a tremendous amount about what successful entrepreneurs do, how they do it, and why. In fact, I would expect that in as early as 2020, as we graduate many more students with proper entrepreneurial training, we will see the failure rate drop dramatically.

Summary

As you have seen, a person may take many different paths to reach the goal of entrepreneurship. You have even learned that sometimes this occurs even if you currently have no interest in becoming an entrepreneur. Based on the unpredictable nature of the different economies around the world, it is sensible for everyone to have at least a basic understanding of the entrepreneurial process, and a good understanding of what it takes to become an entrepreneur. You never know when it might just come in handy.

Chapter 4:

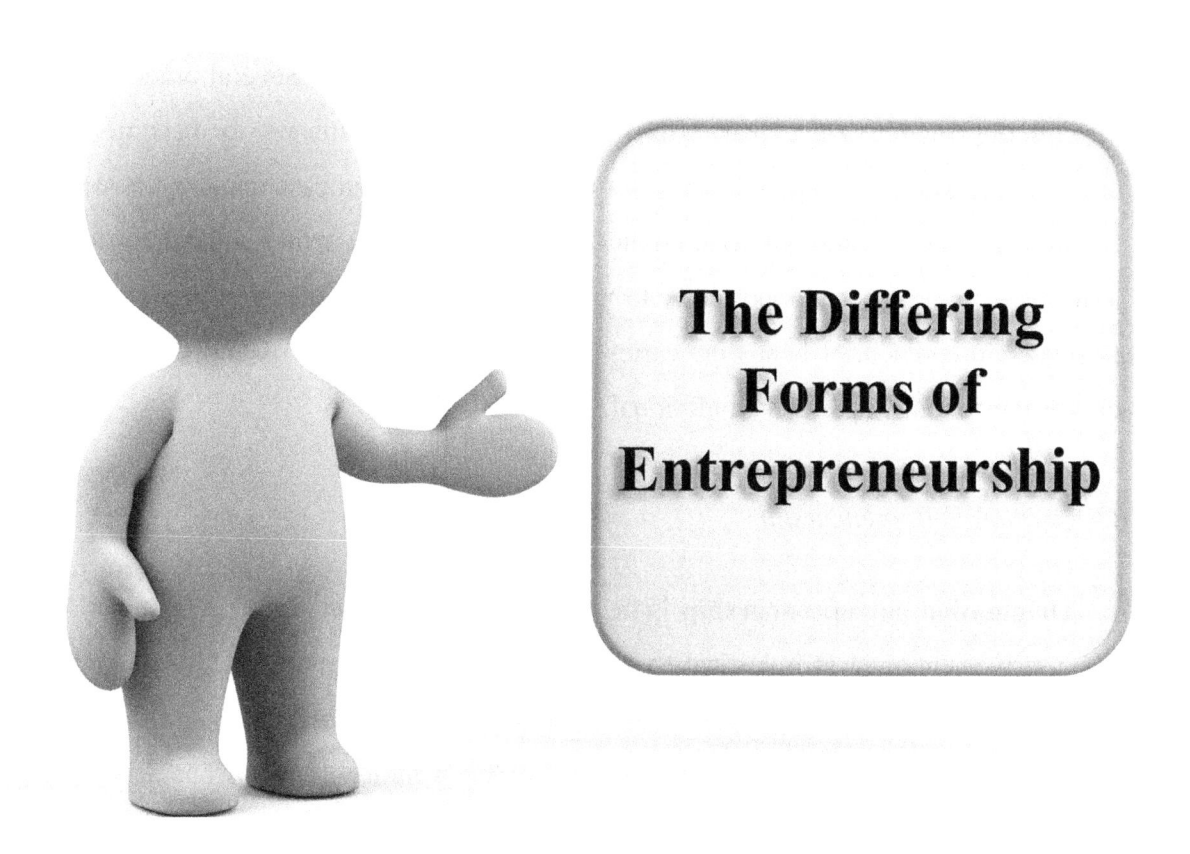

The Differing Forms of Entrepreneurship

As we have discussed in the previous chapters, entrepreneurship is equifinal (can take many different paths to reach the same goal) and may conclude in one of several different possible outcomes or entrepreneurial behaviors based on one's entrepreneurial intentions. In this chapter, we will focus on the different paths you may choose to bring your entrepreneurial opportunities to market.

Forms of Entrepreneurship

Starting a business is not the only form of entrepreneurship. Several other forms of entrepreneurship exist that afford an individual the means to become an entrepreneur. Although the initial part of the entrepreneurial process remains the same for all forms (i.e., locating or creating an entrepreneurial opportunity and determining a means of bringing this opportunity to market), the final part of the entrepreneurial process, entrepreneurial behavior, varies depending on the goal of and the current circumstances surrounding the individual.

Origination Entrepreneurship

Origination entrepreneurship is the act of starting a new venture. However, as previously mentioned, it is critical to understand that just because you start a small business it does not mean you are an entrepreneur. Businesspeople also start businesses. The difference is the uniqueness of the venture. A small business that offers nothing unique, or minimal uniqueness (easily duplicated), is not entrepreneurship. Origination entrepreneurship occurs when an individual locates or creates an entrepreneurial (*unique*) opportunity, evaluates that opportunity to determine if it is feasible (can it be done for a profit) and desirable (is it something they or others want to do). For entrepreneurial behavior relating to origination entrepreneurship to occur, the answer to both the feasibility and desirability questions must be yes. If the answer to the feasibility question is yes, but desirability is no, then the entrepreneur will choose a different form of entrepreneurship to complete the entrepreneurial process. Once a determination is made that a given opportunity is both feasible and desirable, entrepreneurial behaviors relating to starting the business begin. Because *an opportunity may be a product, a process, or a service*, the specific entrepreneurial behaviors will depend on the type of opportunity.

New Product: If the entrepreneurial opportunity is a product, the first consideration in determining behavior becomes whether the product is going to be made and sold (manufactured) or bought and sold (distributed).

If the product is to be *manufactured*, entrepreneurs will typically begin by undertaking traditional business behaviors such as researching the following...

- What equipment is needed to produce the product
- How much room will be needed to house the equipment and store the inventory
- What parts of the product (components) will need to be purchased in order to make and ship the product (raw materials, screws, boxes, etc.)
- Where can the components be purchased for the best price
- What are the skills needed to produce the product
- How many people are going to be needed to produce the product
- How will the product be distributed to the customer (storefront, mail, delivery, etc.)
- How to market the product (this varies radically depending on the customer type)

Once such business research is complete, the entrepreneur then undertakes *entrepreneurial behaviors,* such as determining innovative ways of making the manufacturing process as efficient as possible.

These can include...

- Ways of reducing or eliminating wasted material
- Ways to modify the manufacturing process to reduce the amount of equipment

needed to produce the product (save money on startup cost)
- Ways of producing the product faster while maintaining the quality of the product (This means holding less inventory which saves money on storage costs such as rent and interest)
- Ways of reducing the number of employees needed to produce the product
- Ways of reducing the cost of components (using interchangeable components for multiple products, making some of the components in-house, etc.)

If the product is to be *distributed* (bought and sold), entrepreneurs begin by undertaking much of the same entrepreneurial behaviors previously listed. The difference is entrepreneurs work with their suppliers to determine ways of reducing the cost of the product while maintaining the quality just as they would if they were going to produce the product on their own. Once entrepreneurs have determined the most efficient means of producing or purchasing the product, then and only then, will these entrepreneurs develop a plan for starting and running their business.

New Process: When the entrepreneurial opportunity is a process, the development of the opportunity again has two choices on how to proceed. These are to act as an entrepreneurial consultant or sell the opportunity.

If the new process is a means of utilizing or modifying existing equipment in a novel, more productive manner, in essence streamlining a process, then the focus of exploitation is *entrepreneurial consulting*. Because the entrepreneur has no physical product to sell, only an intellectual one that cannot be protected by a patent or copyright, the best means of exploiting such an opportunity is by contracting their services in a consultant-like manner. Once the entrepreneur's services have been contractually secured, the entrepreneur can then work with the company to modify their process.

If the process consists of utilizing different, currently existing equipment, not previously used in the process, the entrepreneur has two options. One option is to contract with the company as an entrepreneurial consultant, just as in the other scenario, and then show the company what new equipment to buy and how to use it to modify the process. The other more valuable means is to *sell* the details of the new process to the equipment manufacturer. This allows the manufacturer to utilize their existing sales force to do the legwork and the entrepreneur is then free to do other things. In such a scenario the entrepreneur sells the details of the new process to the manufacturer for an upfront fee and, where possible, get a royalty on each unit sold that is produced using the new process. The reason this works for both the entrepreneur and the manufacturer is that in most cases the new utilization of the equipment is often in an entirely new market, a market that the manufacturer was not previously aware existed.

New Service: When the entrepreneurial opportunity is a service, entrepreneurs begin by researching traditional business behaviors of similar services, if they exist, such as...

- *What equipment is needed to provide the service*
- *Where the service is to be provided (client comes to you or you go to them)*
- *If the client comes to you, how much room will be needed to house the equipment and provide the service*
- *If you go to the client, what mode of transportation is needed*
- *What products will be needed or used to provide the service (anything that will be used in providing the service)*
- *Where can these products be purchased for the best price*
- *What are the skills needed to provide the service*
- *How many people are going to be needed to provide the service to everyone who wants it*
- *How to market the product (this varies radically depending on the customer type)*

Following the business research, entrepreneurs then undertake *entrepreneurial behaviors* such as determining innovative ways of providing the service.

These may include...

- Ways of reducing or eliminating wasted product
- Ways of providing additional services to entice the client into additional services
- Ways of reducing the number of employees needed to provide the service
- Ways of reducing the cost of products used (using the same products for multiple services, making some of the products in-house, etc.)

Once entrepreneurs have determined the most efficient means of providing the service, then these entrepreneurs will develop a plan for starting and running their business.

Origination Entrepreneurship Summary

As you can see, origination entrepreneurship may consist of a product, process, or a service; all of which can be produced or provided in many different ways. As a result, entrepreneurs have many different decisions to make regarding how they are going to produce or provide their product, process, or service. The most important of these decisions is always, "How unique can I make it?," because entrepreneurs understand, the more unique it is, the greater the profit will be and for a longer period.

All forms of entrepreneurship begin with locating or creating an entrepreneurial opportunity and determining a means of bringing this opportunity to market. Accordingly, each of the following sections will focus on what is different from origination entrepreneurship. Especially, what these types of entrepreneurs do to locate opportunities (corporate entrepreneurship) or what they do once they locate an entrepreneurial opportunity.

Corporate Entrepreneurship

Corporate entrepreneurship is, for the most part, the same as origination entrepreneurship with one major exception. It takes place within existing traditional businesses. However, corporate entrepreneurship begins with the creation of an environment conducive to entrepreneurship. With this form of entrepreneurship, everyone is encouraged to act like an entrepreneur. This occurs by creating an environment where everyone has the opportunity to become an entrepreneur, within the business. Opportunities are encouraged and welcomed from every employee, from the CEO all the way down to the janitorial staff, and equal consideration given to all. The location or creation of opportunities is not limited to the research and

Chapter 4: The Differing Forms of Entrepreneurship

development department. In such an environment, everyone is encouraged to undertake entrepreneurial behavior, exploring possible entrepreneurial opportunities that work to benefit the business, as well as the individual.

In this environment, ideas can come from existing products, ones that fit within the present scope of the business, or can be a completely new product line, something that has nothing to do with the existing business. Great companies realize the value of a new product and the fallacy of limiting their business to a single type of product (remember the Kodak example in Chapter 2). These companies are more than happy to start a separate division, and in some cases, a completely new company if the opportunity warrants. If this occurs, great companies will actually promote the entrepreneur into a management position within the new company based on the new product, or may even offer part ownership, provided the entrepreneur has the skills and ability to handle the position

This shows how great companies differ from those in the past. In the past, many large corporations fought the idea of diversifying the products they sold until companies like Kodak and IBM showed them the error of their ways by example. Both industry leaders lost major market share by ignoring an emerging product in favor of the status quo and never recovered because of it. The way corporations used to deal with new opportunities, and unfortunately, some still do, was to evaluate an opportunity and see if it fits into their current product line. If it did, then they would effectively give the employee a metaphorical "pat on the head," maybe a small bonus, and say, "now go back to work." If the opportunity did not fit within the sphere of their business type, they would typically ignore the opportunity, and the employee, all together.

Enlightened businesses now see the error of the old ways. Minimal recognition and compensation for the location of a usable opportunity actually works to discourage, not encourage, employees from coming forth when they locate an opportunity. Once a company ends up making any real money from an employee-based opportunity and all that the employee received was a "thanks" and a small bonus, this employee, and any other employee that knows what happened, will keep all future opportunities to themselves. They do this because they fear the company will cheat them out of what they feel is a fair share of the profits. Consequently, such behavior by a company really acts more as an incentive for employees to keep opportunities to themselves and to wait until they can exploit these opportunities on their own.

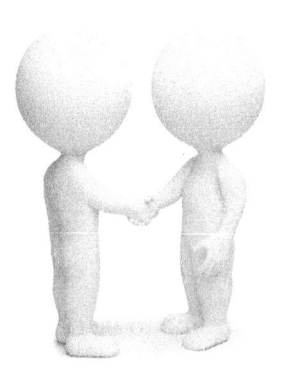

Based on this knowledge, great companies are looking for corporate entrepreneurs, individuals capable of creating an environment within their company that is conducive to entrepreneurial behavior for all employees, effectively creating a company populated by entrepreneurs. One concern from companies considering creating an entrepreneurial environment is the misconception that such an environment of entrepreneurship will become an incubator for new entrepreneurs. Meaning these entrepreneurs will leave the company to start their own businesses. My response to such companies is a simple one. For the vast majority of potential entrepreneurs, the mere thought of failure, and the ensuing consequences (no job, debt, shame, etc.), is enough to keep them from ever trying to start a business on their own. So if these budding entrepreneurs are treated properly (a percentage of the profit, being able to participate if not head the exploitation of the opportunity, and recognition for their accomplishment), why would they ever want to leave? In fact, they are more likely to come up with even more opportunities in the future because this form of entrepreneurship offers them all the rewards of becoming an entrepreneur with none of the risk.

In order to transform a traditional business into an environment conducive to entrepreneurship several things must change. What corporate entrepreneurs do for an existing company is change the environment so that entrepreneurship can occur. They do this initially by creating an environment where tolerance is the norm. This is accomplished by first changing the perception of failure. Failure is a valid way of learning and must not be punished if real learning is to occur. Entrepreneurs are going where no one has gone before. Failure is inevitable and in an entrepreneurial environment means that real effort is taking place. In fact, if the learning is great enough, such failure should actually be rewarded or at least acknowledged as a means of showing the company's commitment to experimentation.

Next, a corporate entrepreneur will encourage employees to take time, often company time, to experiment and try new things. Some companies (e.g., Dow Chemical and 3M) allot a specific amount of time every day for employees to explore entrepreneurial opportunities. Others allow downtime to be used for exploration, instead of what is often referred to as busy work (sweeping or cleaning just to keep an employee busy). Most often, companies simply allow employees to work on their own time, typically before and after their shift, to work on projects. The key, no matter the route, is the use of company equipment and materials. These types of behaviors show employees that the company is serious and willing to commit resources toward the location or creation of entrepreneurial opportunities without demanding specific results.

The creation of this type of entrepreneurial environment within corporations appears to be a real trend, and if it continues, what we are going to be seeing is not entrepreneurship and business as separate but complementary entities, but entrepreneurship as the dominant form of business. This is quite likely to take place due to one resounding fact. The corporate world is finally starting to understand that in this modern global economy, "if you're not growing, you're dying. There is no standing still and entrepreneurship is the answer."

Although origination entrepreneurship and corporate entrepreneurship are currently the predominant forms of entrepreneurship, they are not the only ways an individual can be an entrepreneur. Additional means include commercial and developmental entrepreneurship.

Commercial Entrepreneurship

Commercial entrepreneurs create or locate entrepreneurial opportunities and determine means of exploiting the opportunity just as origination entrepreneurs do. The difference lies in what they do with the opportunity. Instead of creating a business, these entrepreneurs take the opportunity and they sell it. In this circumstance, the entrepreneurs are taking their unique product or service, and coming up with an innovative way of selling or providing the product or service, just as an origination entrepreneur would do. This is where the two differ, a commercial

Chapter 4: The Differing Forms of Entrepreneurship

entrepreneur, unlike an origination entrepreneur, has no interest in starting a particular business. However, because the opportunity has reasonable to significant value for someone who is interested, the entrepreneur can sell the opportunity.

Instead of creating the business, commercial entrepreneurs create a detailed blueprint of the product (or explanation of the service) and a comprehensive plan of how to start and run the business (an entrepreneurial business plan), and proceed to shop around for a buyer. Buyers can consist of individuals who would like to start a unique business, but do not possess the entrepreneurial mindset to locate or create an opportunity on their own. A buyer can also be an existing business that currently sells similar or complementary products or services, or they can even sell them to another entrepreneur who is better suited for the opportunity and simply does not currently have an opportunity to pursue of their own.

The actual sale of an opportunity can take many forms. The opportunity may be sold outright. The opportunity could also be sold for a reduced price, or even given away, with a royalty received on every unit sold or service provided. Ownership of the opportunity may even be retained and the right to produce and sell the product (or provide the service) licensed. The key is the commercial entrepreneur is not profiting from the opportunity by starting a business, but by providing a means for others more suited for the opportunity to do so. This allows the entrepreneur to profit from the opportunity while freeing the entrepreneur up to move on to the next entrepreneurial opportunity.

Developmental Entrepreneurship

Developmental entrepreneurs modify existing businesses or franchises. That is they take something that is already in existence and turn it into something new and unique. A good example for this is fast food franchises. Originally, fast food franchises were all self-standing, independent businesses. At some point, an entrepreneur came up with the idea of doing something different with this concept. Something not previously allowed within the standard franchise model—a fast food mini-restaurant or kiosk. In most cases, this concept would have been rejected immediately. In the past, existing businesses were highly resistant to changing a business model that worked. Nevertheless, at some point, one of the major franchisors must have realized the potential a developmental entrepreneur was proposing because today virtually every gas station has a major fast food mini-restaurant built into it. Something that was not allowed, and frankly unheard of, in the 1980s. This change in the franchise business model likely took a great amount of persistence on the part of a developmental entrepreneur.

Another example is the purchase of an existing business with the intent of converting the current product line to something new and unique. I personally purchased a business in the late 1990s for just such a reason. The company I bought manufactured emergency medical kits, the boxes most emergency medical personnel carry to the scene of an accident. At the time, this company provided 90% of all the emergency medical kits used in the United States. The problem was that this equated to approximately 4000 units a year, with no real growth potential (there are only so many new emergency medical services in the United States every year and, to make it worse, the boxes were virtually indestructible so replacements were rare). In essence, the company was big enough for one person to make a living at, but not much more. My concept was to alter the color (hunter orange), make some modifications to the interior structure, and

Chapter 4: The Differing Forms of Entrepreneurship

sell it as a large, long lasting, high quality tackle box. In the end we offered four different colors and they were available at both of the major mega sporting goods stores. This increased the sales potential of the product tenfold.

The problem with developmental entrepreneurship is the opportunities are often easily replicable, and if you become highly profitable, others will copy what you have done, forcing down your profit. To sufficiently profit from such a developmental opportunity, an entrepreneur must proceed carefully. The entrepreneur must work to secure the sole rights to a large enough region to ensure sufficiently large profits from multiple locations once the franchisor starts to offer the idea to everyone. In the case of a modified business, it may be necessary to secure sole supplier rights for your product at enough major distributors so that when competition comes along they are shut out of a major portion of the market.

Before we continue further, it is important that we address another one of the misconceptions that surround entrepreneurship: that entrepreneurship is a permanent state.

Misconception: Entrepreneurship is a Permanent State

Entrepreneurship is a non-permanent state. By this I mean that once an entrepreneurial opportunity is no longer unique, it is no longer entrepreneurship, it is business. This raises the question, "How long before an entrepreneurial opportunity or venture becomes just another business?" The answer to this question is difficult to answer. Some researchers say the number is somewhere between three and five years. Others use size as a measure. Personally, I hold that it is not the length of time that you are in business, or the number of employees that you have, but rather it depends on the uniqueness of the entrepreneurial opportunity. Some entrepreneurial opportunities have a very short lifespan, meaning that competition exists soon after the opportunity is exploited for the first time (for example, the fast food mini-restaurants). Other opportunities have an *almost* endless lifespan. Either this is due to the high cost of replication or an ability to be protected (e.g., patents, copyright, etc.). However, even these can only be protected so long (patents = 20 years, copyright = life of the creator + 70 years, and so on). The point is that the lifespan of entrepreneurship is dependent on the uniqueness of the opportunity; the more unique the entrepreneurial opportunity, the longer entrepreneurship exists.

Social Entrepreneurship

One of the major misconceptions surrounding social entrepreneurship is that it is a completely independent form of entrepreneurship. Therefore, a key to understanding social entrepreneurship is the realization that all four forms of entrepreneurship, and traditional business (although that would be social business, not social entrepreneurship), can also be socially responsible. Social entrepreneurship is often given other names, such as ecoentrepreneurship, environmental entrepreneurship, and green entrepreneurship, just to name a few. In reality, these are all socially responsible entrepreneurial ventures (social entrepreneurship). The names simply describe the specific area of social responsibility these ventures have chosen to undertake.

Social responsibility is a choice, not an actual form of entrepreneurship or business. In essence, social responsibility is a commitment to society and can take place in one of two ways: 1) A venture can simply take a portion of its profits and commit these profits to be used in a socially responsible manner (helping the less fortunate, preserving buildings of historical value, etc.). 2) A venture can produce a product, utilize a process, or supply a service in a manner that is socially responsible (for example using chemicals that are environmentally safe). Here we will focus on entrepreneurship, although many of these concepts may also pertain to traditional business.

Misconceptions about Social Entrepreneurship: Non-profit

It is important to understand that non-profit does not automatically mean that a business is a truly social venture. Conversely, for-profit does not automatically mean that it is not a social venture. Non-profit, in reality, is nothing more than a legal status, in essence, an agreement with the government to utilize its profits for the betterment of society (be it local, regional, or global). For this commitment, a company receives tax-exempt status. It is the government's way of saying, "if you are going to use *all* your profits to help society, we won't tax you so you will have more to use." However, in most cases, being tax-exempt does make a company a social venture. The reality is that a non-profit may not be as socially responsible as you think.

Under the non-profit status, companies are allowed to award staff, including executives, for improving the company's image, getting donations, etc. This happens at the sole discretion of the board. Thus, it is possible that persons at the top of the venture can end up making an extraordinary amount of money, effectively minimizing the total amount of profit available for the benefit of society. Although this is not the intent of the non-profit status, and not all non-profits abuse this loophole, it is legal. Only if the abuse is considered excessive, and can be proven, will such behavior result in the revocation (loss) of the venture's non-profit status and possible prosecution for tax evasion.

Conversely, for-profit does not automatically mean that a company is not a social venture. For-profit companies have the option of determining how much of its profits it chooses to use for the benefit of society and when. Additionally, for-profit companies may choose to utilize alternate, environmentally safe methods to produce their products or supply their service whether or not it affects their profits. In such an instance, a company may actually increase profits by choosing this method and still honestly claim social responsibility. This is because, when society agrees with what a company is doing to benefit society, it is often willing to pay a premium for the product or service. Thus, any venture that commits to act in a socially responsible manner, whether by its actions or by using profits for the betterment of society, is in fact a social venture, whether it is an entrepreneurship or a traditional business.

Misconceptions about Social Entrepreneurship: Charity

Another major misconception is that charities and social entrepreneurship are the same. In fact, charities are not social entrepreneurship at all. The mandate for social entrepreneurship is the venture must, first and foremost, make a profit (this includes non-profits). Charities do not have such a mandate; they do not make a profit. Next, socially minded entrepreneurial ventures that choose to use their profits for the benefit of society must be self-sustaining. They must function under a business model that allows them to survive without the continued support of benefactors. Although it is becoming a common practice for social entrepreneurship ventures to receive donations from wealthy benefactors or crowd funding to start the venture, these

Chapter 4: The Differing Forms of Entrepreneurship

donations come with the understanding that it is a onetime action to get the venture up and running. A charity's sole means of survival is continuous donations. If the donations stop, the charity dies. This is an important distinction, because a trend appears to be happening. More individuals that used to donate their money to charity are now beginning to hesitate or refuse to give money. The reason is simple. When you donate your money to charity, once the money is gone, they come back for more. When you donate your money to a social venture, what you give starts a reaction that, when handled properly, continues indefinitely without the need for further contributions, thus benefiting society for an indefinite period.

Another possible reason for this migration of benefactors from charities to social ventures might be more personal in nature. Here is a scenario. Say you donate a substantial amount of money, let us say for argument's sake, to a hospital to build a new wing with the sole stipulation that the wing is named after a child you lost far too young, say, "the Matthew Sinclair pediatric wing." In time, inevitably, the wing becomes run down and the equipment out of date. It is in need of repair and updating. Now of course the hospital is going to come to you and ask for more money. However, what happens if you do not have the money to give? Well, they go to someone else. Then what happens to the name (your child's memorial)? If you are lucky, it becomes the "Sinclair-Geczi wing"; if you are not lucky, it becomes the "Geczi wing" and your memorial is lost. Now, if the hospital were a true social venture, a portion of the profits made from this wing would be set aside to ensure the wing is always maintained and the latest equipment always on hand. Your contribution to this social venture would ensure that your memorial lasted for as long as the hospital existed. So which would you choose?

Section 2

The Entrepreneur

Section 1 demonstrated the value and importance of entrepreneurship. From this discussion, you should now understand the important part entrepreneurship plays in society. You should also know exactly what entrepreneurship is and is not. You should understand the different pathways you can take to become an entrepreneur, and the varying reasons people choose to become one. You should know the different forms entrepreneurship can take, and most importantly, in my opinion, why everyone should have a basic understanding of the entrepreneurial process. So now that we have discussed the *who, what, where,* and *when* of entrepreneurship, it is time to change our focus from what entrepreneurship is to what makes a person an entrepreneur—the *how*.

As discussed earlier, entrepreneurs are not born, they are created. For this reason, Section 2 focuses on what makes an entrepreneur unique and what you need to do to prepare yourself for becoming an entrepreneur. Chapter 5 addresses entrepreneurial mindset. Specifically, how entrepreneurs think and what you need to do to start thinking like one. Chapter 6 focuses on creativity—how to prepare your mind to create unique ideas, how to locate new and innovative opportunities, and develop the means of exploiting such opportunities by awakening the creativity within you. Chapter 7 centers on the mental aspects needed to overcome, if not excel, in situations of stress and uncertainty. Essentially, how to survive the inevitable difficulties and failures associated with entrepreneurship. Chapter 8, the final topic of Section 2, talks about the importance of entrepreneurial ethics.

Before continuing, it is important to set a baseline (see where you currently stand as a potential entrepreneur). To that end, please go to the following website and complete the assessment there.

It is extremely important that you answer the questions honestly. If you try to answer the questions the way you think an entrepreneur would, rather than how you really think or feel, you will not get the real answer you are looking for, "Do I have what it takes to become an entrepreneur?"

www.SentreMat.com/eMindset

Please do not worry if you are not happy with your results. You will have the opportunity to take the assessment again at the end of this section once you have learned more about becoming an entrepreneur (your assessment will more than likely improve).

Understanding the Entrepreneurial Process

Before we can talk about the entrepreneur, and what it takes to become one, we must first have an overview of the entrepreneurial process itself. The entrepreneurial process is not a simple and straightforward one, largely because each stage of the process can completely change the perspective of the person going through it. As one enters each stage, new learning takes place. This learning, in turn, affects one's knowledge. New knowledge may require one to re-evaluate one's intentions, and previous intentions are either strengthened or abandoned based on the new information. Simply put, as people learn more about entrepreneurship, either through education or action, they will re-evaluate the strength of their beliefs in their ability to become an entrepreneur, their ability to undertake the specific form of entrepreneurship they have chosen, and their motivation for doing so. This continues throughout the preparation to undertake entrepreneurial behavior and well into the entrepreneurial process itself.

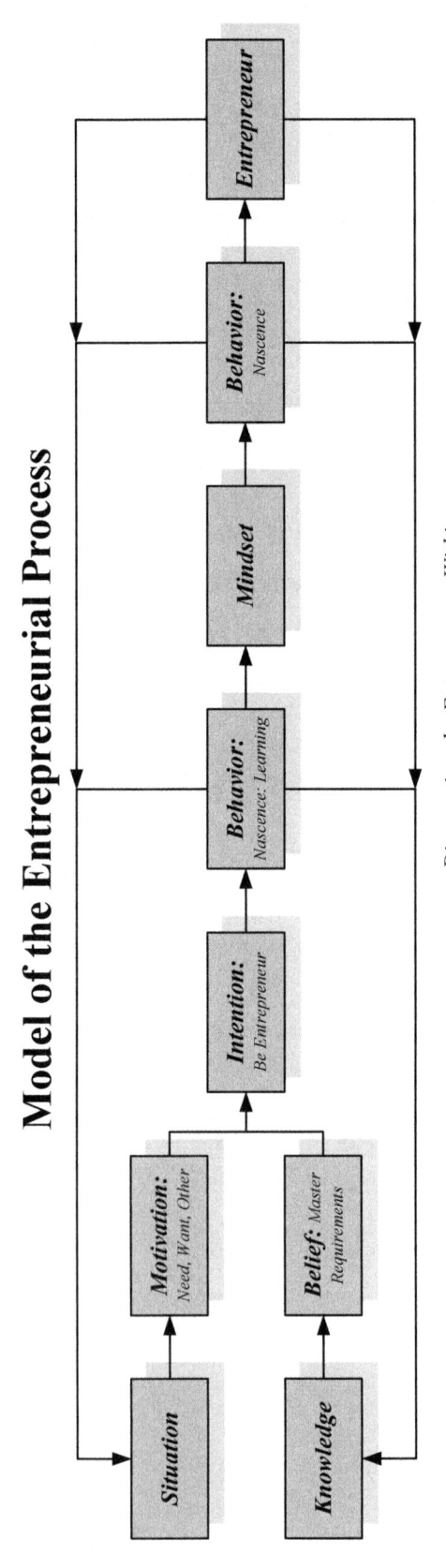

Model of the Entrepreneurial Process

Discovering the Entrepreneur Within

The Entrepreneurial Process

1a. Knowledge of Entrepreneurship

In order to undertake any activity the first thing you need is knowledge relating to that activity. In short, you cannot undertake entrepreneurial behavior if you do not know what entrepreneurship is and what it entails. This you learned in Section 1. However, simply understanding entrepreneurship is not enough to begin the entrepreneurial process—although it is critical for virtually every other step.

1b. Belief in One's Ability to Undertake Entrepreneurial Behavior

Once one understands what entrepreneurship is and is not, the next step in the entrepreneurial process is self-reflection. Based on what you know about yourself, do you believe you could be an entrepreneur? Further explanation will take in place in Chapter 5.

2a. Situation in Relation to Entrepreneurial Behavior

Where you are in your life directly affects your decision to undertake any activity or behavior. With everything else going on in your life (starting a family, buying a house, bills, etc.), can you risk undertaking entrepreneurial behavior?

2b. Motivation to Undertake Entrepreneurial Behavior

Based on one's situation, there are four possible choices, three of which are motivators for undertaking entrepreneurial behavior: 1) *need based,* entrepreneurship is the best possible means of taking care of oneself and their family; 2) *want based,* entrepreneurship is a career choice; 3) *opportunity based*, one has come across an entrepreneurial opportunity too good to pass up; or 4) one chooses a different career path. More discussion on these choices will take place in the introduction to Section 3.

3. Intention to Undertake Entrepreneurial Behavior

Built from a combination of one's beliefs about one's ability to undertake entrepreneurial behavior (1b) and one's motivation to undertake entrepreneurial behavior (2b) a person either will (choices 1, 2, or 3) or will not (choice 4) form an intention to become an entrepreneur. This intention leads one to begin undertaking entrepreneurial behaviors relating to learning more about the specific form of entrepreneurship one is interested in (step 4) or to rule out entrepreneurship as a possibility. We will discuss more about this in the introduction to Section 3.

4. Entrepreneurial Behavior: Learning (Nascence)

Until one has personally undertaken a given behavior, one's knowledge of that behavior (no matter how vast), is limited to what one has learned thus far. What is missing is the experience that comes with actually undertaking a given behavior. In entrepreneurship, this is further complicated by the fact there are several different forms of entrepreneurship, as we have learned in Section 1. Consequently, the beliefs that lead a person to form the intention to become an entrepreneur may change at any given time during the process of learning the knowledge, skills, and ability needed for the specific form of entrepreneurship chosen. In short, as you learn more about what it takes to become the type of entrepreneur you think you want to be, you may change your mind and decide entrepreneurship is not for you.

5. Formation of an Entrepreneurial Mindset

Once one has amassed a sufficient amount of information relating to the specific form of entrepreneurship one would like to undertake, one begins to form a mindset, the topic of Chapter 5. The formation of an entrepreneurial mindset changes entrepreneurial behavior from learning how to become a specific type of entrepreneur (Step 4), to the location or creation of an entrepreneurial opportunity, and the best possible means of exploiting that opportunity (Step 6).

6. Entrepreneurial Behavior: Opportunity Location or Creation and Exploitation

Even though entrepreneurial behavior has shifted to the location or creation of an entrepreneurial opportunity, and a suitable means of exploitation, this is rarely an easy task. However, entrepreneurs typically use one of several methods that exist to assist in locating or creating such opportunities (see Chapter 9). Once a suitable opportunity has been located, entrepreneurial behavior then entails the evaluation of the opportunity's feasibility and desirability (Chapter 10). Provided that the opportunity is feasible, entrepreneurial behavior changes to the formal creation of a plan of action (entrepreneurial business plan). If the opportunity is feasible but not desirable, this plan focuses on how one may exploit the opportunity and whom that person or corporation might be in order to sell the opportunity. If the opportunity is both feasible and desirable, the plan focuses on how the nascent entrepreneur will personally exploit the opportunity.

Remember, the beliefs that lead a person to form the intention to become an entrepreneur may change at any given time throughout the process. For example, if one is unable to locate or create an entrepreneurial opportunity, or unable to determine a means of exploiting a located opportunity, or one's situation and thus one's motivation to become an entrepreneur changes (e.g., a job that is just too good to pass up, children, etc.) they may change their mind. For these individuals entrepreneurship is no longer right for them—at least not at this time.

7. Entrepreneurship

Finally, it is important to remember that entrepreneurship is not a permanent state naturally. Traditionally, entrepreneurship at some point stops being entrepreneurship and simply becomes business. For entrepreneurship to continue indefinitely the entrepreneur must either create an entrepreneurial environment, one of continuous creativity and innovation, or continue to locate or create new entrepreneurial opportunities as the old ones become simple businesses. Additionally, entrepreneurs may re-evaluation their intention to be entrepreneurs based on their experiences and choose to seek different career paths (whether their entrepreneurial endeavors were successful or not).

Conclusion

Now that you have a basic understanding of the entrepreneurial process, we can focus on the specifics of what makes an entrepreneur unique and what you need to do to prepare yourself for becoming an entrepreneur.

Chapter 5:

Entrepreneurial Mindset

In order to answer the question, "how does one become an entrepreneur?", we must first start with how an entrepreneur thinks—the entrepreneur's mindset.

In Chapter 1, we discussed the three components necessary for entrepreneurship to take place. These are an entrepreneurial mindset, the motivation to act, and an opportunity. Although all three are critical to the entrepreneurial process, the entrepreneurial mindset is often the most difficult to comprehend. Therefore, this chapter is devoted to the concept of entrepreneurial mindset.

Mindset

What is a *mindset*? We hear the term used all the time. For example, "He really has his *mind set* on going to the game" or "She really has her *mind set* on becoming a doctor." From these examples, we can see that mindset is a type of focus aimed at a

Discovering the Entrepreneur Within

specific outcome, object, or state. This focus can vary in range from a slight preoccupation to an outright obsession. For our purpose, the object of mindset relates to entrepreneurship. Like all mindsets, entrepreneurial mindset also varies in intensity from a simple preoccupation, or curiosity about entrepreneurship, to an outright obsession with becoming an entrepreneur. This is why it has been difficult for academics to agree on what an entrepreneurial mindset truly is and how, or why, it develops in any given entrepreneur. To start, it is important to define exactly what entrepreneurial mindset means.

Entrepreneurial Mindset

Although several definitions exist, when combined they suggest that an entrepreneurial mindset is a way of thinking that allows a person to locate or create entrepreneurial opportunities and determine the best possible means of exploiting such opportunities. Based on this description, we can see that entrepreneurial mindset has two primary components, 1) the location or creation of an entrepreneurial opportunity and 2) the location or creation of a means to exploit that opportunity. What these components have in common are the act of *location* and *creation*, or in terms that are more specific, **alertness** and **creativity**. Therefore, for our purposes, we will define an entrepreneurial mindset as follows...

> **Entrepreneurial mindset** *is a heightened sensitivity to opportunities that have entrepreneurial potential (**alertness**) and the ingenuity to create, modify, or adapt (**creativity**) these opportunities in such a way as to allow the entrepreneur to profit from the opportunity, often when others cannot.*

Chapter 5: Entrepreneurial Mindset

So how does one come to possess an entrepreneurial mindset? After all, we know that entrepreneurs are not born with one.

An entrepreneurial mindset is a mental state developed over time. For many entrepreneurs it took years for them to develop their entrepreneurial mindset. They did this by honing their skills and abilities to the point that the use of their entrepreneurial mindset is second nature. This is the reason that many existing entrepreneurs believe entrepreneurship is not teachable, but must be lived or experienced in order to learn. They believe this because it is something they learned over a long period, through trial and error, and do not see any other way it could be learned. However, like any learning process, it is possible to accelerate the development of a mindset, once you know how and are truly willing to put forth the effort. To begin, we need to understand the cognitive mechanisms behind entrepreneurial mindset.

Creating an Entrepreneurial Mindset

Knowledge of Entrepreneurship

In order to form any mindset the first thing you need is knowledge relating to that mindset. In short, you cannot form an entrepreneurial mindset until you know what entrepreneurship truly is. This is why so many people call themselves entrepreneurs when, in fact, they are really inventors or businesspeople. Misinformation regarding entrepreneurship is another problem. Because of such misinformation, (e.g., that in order to be an entrepreneur you must start a business or that 50% of all entrepreneurial ventures fail) many people do not consider a career as an entrepreneur.

Since many entrepreneurs formed their mindset over a long period through trial and error, the first section of this book focused on understanding what is and is not entrepreneurship to help speed up the mindset formation process. However, simply understanding what is and is not entrepreneurship is not enough to begin the formation process—although it is critical to the second step.

Belief in One's Ability to Become an Entrepreneur

Once one understands what entrepreneurship is, the next step in the mindset formation process is self-reflection. The entrepreneurial mindset forms as the result of three distinct ways of thinking that relate to how people think about or believe in themselves. These are: **entity schema** (how one thinks people acquire knowledge, skills, and abilities); **possible self-concept** (how one thinks about the possibility of undertaking a given behavior); and **self-efficacy** (how one thinks about overcoming unknown obstacles in life). All three ways of thinking play a specific role in the formation of an entrepreneurial mindset based on one's knowledge of entrepreneurship and the entrepreneurial process.

Entity Schema. There are two distinctly different entity schemas. These are a static entity schema and a dynamic entity schema. Although as many as 95% of all people display a strong tendency toward one or the other of these entity schema, it is not a simple one or the other proposition. In fact, it is more like a sliding scale with static entity schema on one side and dynamic entity schema on the other.[1]

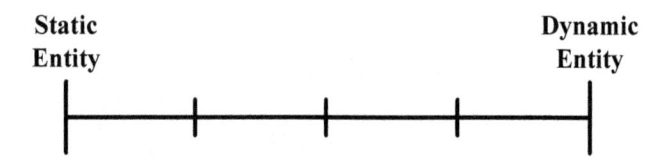

```
       Static                            Dynamic
       Entity                            Entity
       |-------|-------|-------|-------|
```

What these two schemas have in common is the focus on *how one acquires knowledge, skills, and abilities*. In the simplest of terms, individuals possessing a static entity schema believe learning is an inborn trait and those with a dynamic entity schema believe learning is the result of effort. Now, it is not important who is right and who is wrong. What is important is how each affects the development of entrepreneurial mindset.

Static entity schema, also referred to as a fixed[2] or helplessness[3] mindset, is the belief that the ability to learn is an inherent or genetic characteristic, and as such, unchangeable.[4] Individuals with this schema see themselves as born with or somehow having a natural ability that is beyond their control. Any attempt to exceed their current capacities is seen as being fruitless and often limits such individuals' ability for personal growth. Based on this understanding, it is easy to see that individuals with a static entity schema are unlikely to become entrepreneurs. The exception to this statement would be individuals who believe they are naturally gifted, or born,

---

[1] Dweck, C. S. (2000). *Self-Theories: Their Role in Motivation, Personality, and Development (Essays in Social Psychology)*. Philadelphia: Psychology Press.

[2] Dweck, C. S. (1996). Implicit theories as organizers of goals and behavior. In P. M. Gollwitzer, & J. A. Bargh (Eds.), *The Psychology of Action: Cognition and Motivation to Behavior*. New York: Guilford Press, 69-90.

[3] Dweck, C. S. (1975). The role of expectations and attributions in the alleviation of learned helplessness. *Journal of Personality & Social Psychology* 31(4): 674-685.

[4] Dweck, C. S. (2006). *Mindset: The New Psychology of Success*. New York: Random House.

with entrepreneurial abilities. It is important to understand that a static entity schema is not the same as low self-esteem or pessimism. In fact, individuals with a static entity schema are often just as confident, optimistic, and positive, even to the point of arrogance,[1] as individuals with a dynamic entity schema.

Dynamic entity schema, also known as a mastery-oriented,[5] malleable,[6] or growth mindset[4] is the belief that one's abilities or accomplishments are largely the result of hard work. Natural ability is seen as, at best, an advantage to be built upon, not a primary determinant of success. Another difference between those individuals with a static entity schema and those with a dynamic entity schema, as it relates to entrepreneurial mindset, is the perception of failure. Individuals with a static-entity schema see failure as a direct reflection on who they are personally, rather than on the state of their current knowledge, skill, and ability. For example, to someone with a static entity schema, the failure of a business is a sign of ignorance or incompetence, rather than as a sign of poor preparation or bad timing. As a result, individuals with a static entity schema tend to spend time trying to avoid situations where they might fail, rather than spending time trying to ensure their success.

Given what we now know, it is easy to see why most individuals with a static entity schema will not likely possess an entrepreneurial mindset due to a strong aversion to the possibility of failure. The good news for those individuals who currently possess a static entity schema, and wish to become entrepreneurs, is that research has shown that a static entity schema does not have to be a permanent state—*it can change.*

---

[5] Diener, C. I., & Dweck, C. S. (1980). An analysis of learned helplessness: II. The processing of success. *Journal of Personality & Social Psychology* 39(5): 940-952.

[6] Elliott, E. S., & Dweck, C. S. (1988). Goals: An approach to motivation and achievement. *Journal of Personality and Social Psychology* 54(1): 5.

In contrast to those with a static entity schema, individuals with a dynamic entity schema see failure not as a reflection on who they are but as a lack of preparation and often even an opportunity to learn. This is not to say that individuals with a dynamic entity schema are unaffected by failure. On the contrary, research has shown these individuals to be just as affected by significant failure as those with a static entity schema.[1] The difference lies in their ultimate response to failure. Those with a static entity schema tend to avoid further activities for which failure has occurred. Those with a dynamic entity schema, after an appropriate time for self-reflection and doubt, focus on determining the reason for failure and implementing a strategy for future success.

Based on these important differences, it is easy to see that individuals with an entrepreneurial mindset are much more likely to possess a dynamic entity schema than a static entity schema. Note: This does not mean that everyone with a dynamic entity schema has, or will develop, an entrepreneurial mindset. All it means is those individuals who possess a dynamic entity schema have one of the primary components necessary for an entrepreneurial mindset to develop.

How is a dynamic entity schema important to the formation of entrepreneurial mindset?

Because the basic nature of entrepreneurship is the act of creating something that is unique, it inherently comes with an amount of uncertainty not typically associated with other careers. Such uncertainty comes from the impossibility of knowing everything that one needs to know in order to exploit a given opportunity. For most careers, new entrants have people within the business to help guide them through the early stages. This guidance serves to minimize uncertainty by reducing the possibility and fear of failure through the knowledge that someone will be there who has the answers to any questions that may arise. Entrepreneurs, however, rarely have such support. Entrepreneurs are blazing their own trails and must be able to overcome all unknown obstacles as they meet them. A dynamic entity schema permits entrepreneurs to look at failure differently by providing them the confidence that they can learn anything they need to know along the way, thus reducing the fear of failure.

In short, a dynamic entity schema provides individuals with the confidence in their ability to learn needed information as they go, thus reducing the possibility and fear of failure. Additionally, the fear of failure is minimal because, should failure occur, a dynamic entity schema gives these individuals the ability to learn from their failures rather than run from them. The next component needed in the formation of an entrepreneurial mindset is that of self-concept.

Possible Entrepreneurial Self-Concept

In general, **self-concept** is how people see themselves, and it helps to organize and process self-relevant information.[7] Self-concept includes the things people rate

---

[7] Markus, H. R. (1977). Self-schemata and processing information about the self. *Journal of Personality and Social Psychology* 35(2): 63-78.

themselves highly on, without doubt,[8] which creates the **current self**, and focuses on who a person aspires to become, as well as whom they fear they may become, the **possible self**.[9] When taken as a whole, the two act to interpret and organize a person's actions and experiences, including consequences, into specific behaviors in response to the social environment.[10] These two perceptions are determined based on four unique sub-dimensions. They are intellectual,[11] social, emotional, and physical self-concepts.[12]

Intellectual Self. Entrepreneurial behavior does not require a degree or any formal education. We all know that people have become successful entrepreneurs without virtually any formal education. For example, Andrew Carnegie, industrialist and one of the first multi-millionaires, dropped out of elementary school. Benjamin Franklin, inventor, scientist, and author, was self-taught. Dave Thomas, founder of Wendy's™, dropped out of high school at 15. George Eastman, founder of Kodak™, dropped out of high school. Richard Branson, founder of Virgin Records™, Virgin Mobile™, and much more, dropped out of high school at age 16. These are but a few examples of the many people who have become successful entrepreneurs without the benefits of a formal education. What all these entrepreneurs have in common is the belief that each

---

[8] Fiske, S. T. (2004). *Social Beings: A Core Motives Approach to Social Psychology*. Hoboken, New Jersey: John Wiley & Sons.

[9] Markus, H. R., & Nurius, P. (1986). Possible selves. *American Psychologist* 41(9): 954-969.

[10] Markus, H. R., & Wurf, E. 1987. The dynamic self-concept: A social psychological perspective. *Annual Reviews in Psychology* 38(1): 299-337.

[11] Sinclair, R.F. (2012). Unpublished dissertation, University of Louisville.

[12] Shavelson, R. J., & Bolus, R. (1982). Self-concept: The interplay of theory and methods. *Journal of Educational Psychology* 74(1): 3-17.

was intelligent enough to undertake entrepreneurial behavior despite their academic achievements or lack thereof. For that reason, a person must believe they are smart enough to undertake entrepreneurship in order for them to be able to see themselves as capable of becoming an entrepreneur.

Social Self. Entrepreneurial behavior often requires a high degree of social interaction (e.g., dealing with customers, employees, vendors, bankers, etc.). Additionally, entrepreneurs rarely possess all the knowledge and experience needed to recognize and exploit a given entrepreneurial opportunity.[13] As a result, entrepreneurs need to have social networks in areas of weakness that augment their own knowledge and experience, referred to as **social capital**.[14] Therefore, those individuals who believe they possess the social skills necessary for entrepreneurial behavior are more likely to form an entrepreneurial mindset. For that reason, people must believe they are capable of creating the social interactions needed for entrepreneurship in order for them to be able to see themselves as capable of becoming entrepreneurs.

Emotional Self. Entrepreneurship, at least in the beginning, typically creates a lot of anxiety and stress. Long hours, pressure from people (and yourself), problems with almost everything you plan, frustrations, and limitations, all act to create an

---

[13] Baron, R. A. (2010). Job design and entrepreneurship: Why closer connections= mutual gains. *Journal of Organizational Behavior* 31(2 3): 370-378.

[14] De Carolis, D. M., & Saparito, P. (2006). Social capital, cognition, and entrepreneurial opportunities: A theoretical framework. *Entrepreneurship Theory and Practice* 30(1): 41-56.

environment that is fraught with uncertainty, doubt, and fear. Since such stressors exist with becoming an entrepreneur, one must be capable of handling the personal, social, and cultural stress associated with entrepreneurial behavior.[15,16] Consequently, the ability to remain emotionally strong in stressful situations, and to rebound from failure if it occurs, is extremely important to the formation of entrepreneurial mindset. Without such emotional strength, individuals often end entrepreneurial behavior at the first sign of difficulty in favor of more pleasurable or comfortable behavior.[17] Due to the highly stressful nature of entrepreneurial behavior, individuals who are likely to form an entrepreneurial mindset are those who do not fear stressful situations and may even thrive on such situations. That is why people must believe they are emotionally capable of handling the known stressors of entrepreneurship in order for them to be able to see themselves as being capable of becoming an entrepreneur.

Physical Self. Because the physical self is dependent on the specific form of entrepreneurial behavior, the only requirement from this dimension is one's ability to see no physical limitation that relates to the specific form of entrepreneurial behavior that might be undertaken. However, because the physical self represents two distinct aspects: perception of one's body and its fundamental abilities,[18] body image can be

---

[15] Lau, B., Hem, E., et al. (2006). Personality types, coping, and stress in the Norwegian Police Service. *Personality and Individual Differences* 41(5): 971-982.

[16] Ensley, M. D., Pearce, C. L., et al. (2006). The moderating effect of environmental dynamism on the relationship between entrepreneur leadership behavior and new venture performance. *Journal of Business Venturing* 21(2): 243-263.

[17] Shavelson, R. J., & Bolus, R. (1982). Self-concept: The interplay of theory and methods. *Journal of Educational Psychology*, 74(1): 3-17.

[18] Shavelson, R. J., Hubner, J. J., & Stanton, G. C. (1976). Self-concept: validation of construct interpretations. *Review of Educational Research*, 46: 407-441.

just as important as physical ability in the formation of an entrepreneurial possible self. For example, if one is starting a unique business related to physical fitness, expectations exist that individuals related to the venture should themselves be physically fit. To that end, only those who see themselves as physically fit are likely to believe they are physically capable of becoming this type of entrepreneur. Another example would be individuals interested in entrepreneurial behavior relating to beauty. If these individuals do not see themselves as being physically attractive, they are unlikely to believe they are capable of becoming this type of entrepreneur.

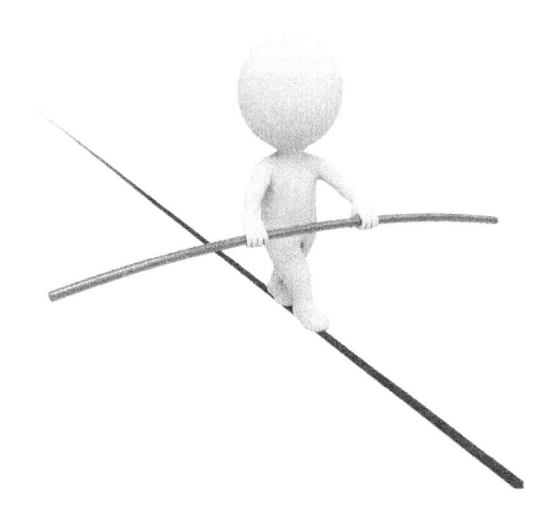

Additionally, if the form of entrepreneurial behavior requires personal interaction with persons previously unknown, those with a substandard body image are likely to avoid the physical interactions necessary to this form of entrepreneurial behavior. Such cognitive dissonance, the conflict between what individuals want and what they feel they are capable of,[19] results in stress. Due to this aspect, the physical self can also have a direct effect on one's social and emotional self-perceptions. Therefore, people must believe they are capable, in both appearance and ability, of physically undertaking the specific form of entrepreneurship they are interested in, before they are able to see themselves as entrepreneurs.

To summarize, an entrepreneurial possible self, the capacity for one to imagine oneself as one day becoming an entrepreneur, comes from the belief that one is intellectually, socially, emotionally, and physically capable of undertaking the

---

[19] Bercovitz, J., & Feldman, M. (2008). Academic entrepreneurs: Organizational change at the individual level. *Organization Science* 19(1): 69-89.

specific form of entrepreneurial behavior of interest. Should they decide to one day become an entrepreneur.

Why is being able to see yourself as an entrepreneur important to the formation of entrepreneurial mindset?

Seeing entrepreneurship as plausible creates incentive for future entrepreneurial behavior. Consequently, more attention and stronger emotional reactions are given to events that are relevant to becoming an entrepreneur, specifically favoring events that support the desired transition from what one is doing now to becoming an entrepreneur.[9] Quite simply, if you cannot see yourself as becoming an entrepreneur, why would you try? The final component needed in the formation of an entrepreneurial mindset is that of self-efficacy.

Self-Efficacy

Efficacy is one's power to create a given outcome. **Self-efficacy** is the *strength of one's belief* in one's ability to create a given outcome, and this belief operates partially independent of underlying skill.[20,21,22] In short, self-efficacy is your belief, whether accurate or not, that you can make things happen, even when you know you do not currently have the skill or ability to do so. This form of willpower can be a significant determinant of performance, although not always positive. Consequently, people with high self-efficacy often view a difficult or seemingly impossible task as something that requires mastering rather than something to avoid. However, an excess of self-efficacy can actually be detrimental; overconfidence in

---

[20] Bandura, A. (1977). Self-efficacy: Toward a unifying theory of behavioral change. *Psychological Review* 84(2): 191-215.
[21] Bandura, A. (1982). Self-efficacy mechanism in human agency. *American Psychologist* 37(2): 122-147.
[22] Bandura, A. (1986). *Social Foundations of Thought and Action: A Social Cognitive Theory*. Englewood Cliffs, New Jersey: Prentice-Hall.

one's self-efficacy can lead one to be less likely to put forth the effort necessary to create a given outcome.

Although similar, self-efficacy and self-concept are not the same. They differ in method of formation. Self-concepts are *objective*, or fact based, beliefs about one's self, based primarily on specific personal aspects (I know I can); whereas self-efficacy is a *subjective*, or opinion based, belief in one's perception (I think I can). For example, one's belief of being capable of starting a business is the result of self-concept when the individual has previous experience starting a business. In essence, *I know I can because I have before*. When one thinks one can start businesses, but has never started a business before, this is the result of self-efficacy. In this instance, *I think I can because of who I am*.

Self-efficacy forms based on one's prior and observed experiences, and through social persuasion. These three act together to build self-efficacy by using reason, inference, and encouragement to build one's perception of one's ability to conquer the unknown.

Prior Experience. The general perception is that prior success acts to raised perceived self-efficacy, whereas failure tends to lower it.[20] This may not always be accurate. The perception is that that early failure, especially if not attributable to a lack of preparation, effort, or unforeseen external influences, could substantially lower one's perceived self-efficacy by leaving one feeling unable to accurately judge one's own abilities, thus lowering self-efficacy. Although this statement is accurate for individuals possessing a static entity schema, this is not necessarily the case with individuals possessing a dynamic entity schema. Remember, individuals possessing a dynamic entity schema tend to see failure as a learning experience.

Chapter 5: Entrepreneurial Mindset

Based on this, a single failure would not have a substantial effect on self-efficacy if it is attributable to a lack of preparation or effort.

Another possible misconception is that failure, following a string of successes, is likely to have minimal effect, as individuals are likely to attribute the failure to lack of preparation, insufficient effort, or situational factors, rather than to ability. Again, this statement is not necessarily accurate. It is true that individuals possessing a dynamic entity schema are likely to see a single failure as attributable to a lack of preparation, or effort, or as an anomaly, and as such, have little or no effect on their self-efficacy. In fact, it is even possible that such a failure could raise one's self-efficacy by allowing such individuals to feel confident in their ability to avoid future failure. However, because individuals possessing a static entity schema see all failure as a reflection on ability, even failure due to circumstances beyond their control, any failure would result in a substantial reduction of self-efficacy. Based on this refinement of self-efficacy perception, a dynamic entity schema has not only a direct effect on perception, but also an effect on the relationship between prior experience and one's perception of self-efficacy. Self-efficacy is not only formed through prior experience, it can also be obtained through perceived efficacy of similar phenomena.[21]

Observed Experience. Self-efficacy can also be obtained through the observation of others.[20] By observing how others perform in given situations, and through comparison of one's own perceived abilities to those observed, it is possible to *infer* one's ability to perform a given behavior.[21] For example, if a friend were to start a successful venture and one's perception is that this friend's ability is no greater than one's own, this perception would likely raise one's perceived self-efficacy.[23] In this instance, the observed experience of others creates the perception that *if others can do it, so can I*. Conversely, it is just as possible that observed failure of others, with perceived ability equal to one's own, could act to reduce self-efficacy.

Although observed experiences generally have a weaker effect on self-efficacy than personal experience,[22] these observations may have a significant impact on one's willingness to persist at a given behavior. For example, if you observe successful entrepreneurs with perceived abilities not greater than your own, and you are not currently doing well with your own attempt, these observations may motivate you to continue longer and try harder by bolstering your effort. In essence this situation creates the perception, *if others can do it, I know I can too if I just work a little harder.*

Social Persuasion. The formation of self-efficacy is not limited to prior and observed experiences with a given phenomenon. Self-efficacy can also form through **social persuasion**. That is, the attempts of others to convince individuals they possess, or do not possess, the ability to succeed. While "social persuasion alone may be limited in its power to create enduring increases in self-efficacy"[22,p.400], it may act

---

[23] Shapero, A. (1984). The entrepreneurial event. In C. A. Kent (Ed.), *The Environment for Entrepreneurship*. Lexington, Massachusetts: Lexington Books, 21-40.

as a much needed boost in times of self-doubt. However, social persuasion can have a much greater effect when used to undermine one's self-efficacy. This is because those who have been convinced of self-inefficacy are more likely to avoid that specific behavior, or give up quickly in the face of difficulty, fearing impending failure as confirmation of self-inefficacy. In essence, socially induced self-inefficacy encourages one to move toward a static entity schema.

Why is self-efficacy important to the formation of entrepreneurial mindset?

Self-efficacy is important to the formation of an entrepreneurial mindset because it provides one with *the will* to persist under uncertain and difficult conditions. Additionally, self-efficacy allows one to see obstacles as a challenge rather than a barrier to avoid. Both are abilities necessary for continuation of the entrepreneurial process.

In summary to answer the question, how does one come to possess an entrepreneurial mindset?

1. One must know what is and is not entrepreneurship *(Knowledge)*.
2. One must have a reason to become an entrepreneur *(Motivation)*.
3. One must believe one is capable of becoming an entrepreneur *(Possible Self)*.
4. One must believe one is capable of learning whatever one does not know along the way *(Dynamic Entity Schema and Intellectual Self)*.
5. One must believe one is able to handle failure and learn from it *(Emotional Self and Dynamic Entity Schema)*.
6. One must believe one is able to handle the uncertainty, and often fear, that comes with entrepreneurial behavior *(Dynamic Entity Schema, Possible Self, and Self-Efficacy)*.
7. One must believe that one is capable of overcoming any obstacle that may arise when attempting to undertake entrepreneurial behavior *(Self-Efficacy)*.

Only once all these conditions exist will an entrepreneurial mindset form.

Chapter 6:

Creativity and Innovation

In our discussion of the entrepreneur, one of the major topics to repeat itself is that entrepreneurs must be creative. This chapter focuses on what creativitiy is and how one goes about unleashing the creative person inside.

Creativity and Innovation

What Are Creativity and Innovation and How Do They Differ?

Creation is the act of bringing something completely new and valuable into existence. **Innovation** refers to the use of something that exists in a better, more valuable or productive way. This differs from the concept of **improvement**. Whereas innovation is doing something different, improvement is doing something better. To help with understanding the differences, let us use the telephone as an example.

- **Creation**   *Cell phone entirely different from the home phone (landline)*
- **Innovation**   *Adding a calendar, calculator, and contacts to a cell phone*
- **Improvement**   *Making better versions of the calendar, calculator, and contacts*

Why Does it Matter What Form I Choose?

First, and foremost, it matters to you as a potential entrepreneur. Although this may seem a little off topic, to understand why creativity and innovation matter to entrepreneurs you have to first understand one of the basic principles of markets—competition.

If one creates an entirely new, unique product, process, or service no competition exists. Consequently, an entrepreneur is able to make above average profits for an extended period, either through means of legal protection (patent, copyright, etc.) or because it takes time for the competition to catch up. How long the entrepreneur can make above average profits depends on how unique the product, process, or service is and how difficult it is to duplicate. As a result, the more unique the product, process, or service, the longer the entrepreneur can make above average profits. Therefore, quite simply, if it is entrepreneurship, one can expect above average profits because competition does not exist. If it is business, one can only expect average profits because competition will exist almost immediately. With this in mind, we can return to our discussion of creativity and innovation.

The basic rule of thumb is that creation is virtually always entrepreneurship; innovation may or may not be entrepreneurship; and improvement is virtually never entrepreneurship. Therefore, it is important to entrepreneurs that they seek the most creative opportunities possible.

Creativity, as it pertains to entrepreneurship, focuses on bringing something completely new into existence. However, it is important to understand that just because something is new, that does not automatically mean it is unique and as such offers above average profits for an extended period. For example, a new item that is quite similar in nature to another item does not automatically create the uniqueness necessary for above average profits for an extended period. The reason for this is alternatives. Again, a good example of alternatives is the cell phone.

Although today we cannot imagine not having our own personal communication devices, when it was first offered to the general public back in the early 1980s the cell phone received little attention. This is because of the alternative. Virtually everyone already had a home phone (landline) and the price of having one was reasonable. On the other hand, the cell or car phone as they were called (because they were so big the vast majority had to be installed into a car), were seen as an expensive luxury. Thus, most people, even though they really liked the idea, opted for the alternative, to stay with the reasonable priced home phone. Only once competition existed, causing the price to drop, did the cell phone become widely adopted by the average person. This is a good example of a new and unique product that was unable to receive above average profits for an extended period due to the alternatives. If people had not had an alternative, and they really needed the product, process, or service, this would not have been the case.

Therefore, something to keep in mind as one looks to create or locate entrepreneurial opportunities or the means to exploit them is, does the product, process, or service have alternatives that may cause people not to buy it. If this is the case, you have to determine the price point at which people are willing to choose your product, process, or service over the alternative. However, this is the exception, not the rule. Most products, processes, or services that are truly new and unique do afford the entrepreneur above average profits for an extended period. How long depends on how unique it is. The more unique the product, process, or service, the longer the entrepreneur can expect to make above average profits.

Innovation, once again as it pertains to entrepreneurship, refers to the use of something that currently exists in a better, more valuable, or productive way. In our discussions of entrepreneurship and the entrepreneur, you may have noticed that we always use the terms locate and create together. This is because entrepreneurship can occur either through the act of creation, as we have just discussed, or through the act of location. When we talk about location, we are most often referring to innovation.

It is quite common for entrepreneurs to locate a product, process, or service that someone else has already created. Often what happens in these situations is the entrepreneur sees a use that the inventor or businessperson did not. It is this insight that affords the entrepreneur the opportunity to create a unique entrepreneurial opportunity. Yet again, if we use the cell phone example, we can see how this can occur. In the 1980s small personal electronic devices really took off. One of these devices, the PDA (the personal digital assistant), was a great little device, the size of a current cell phone, which allowed one to store large amounts of information and carry it with one at all times. Most PDAs allowed one to keep contact information for all of the people and businesses one knew and dealt with. In addition, one could use it as a personal calendar complete with reminders of what one needed to do and when. Such devices even had a calculator function. This meant that a person no longer needed to carry an address book, a travel calendar, and a calculator with them at all times. In fact, for many businesspersons, it removed the need for a briefcase all together. Now you may say, "Wait a minute, all of that is available on my cell phone"—exactly. What you need to understand is that in the mid 1980s the cell phone was nothing more than a portable house phone. The only feature these cell phones had was very limited contact storage ability. You could store a number and a name; that is all. This is where innovation comes into play. Someone, most likely an entrepreneur, realized that combining a PDA and a cell phone could increase the value of both by reducing or eliminating their alternatives. After all, the cell phone would theoretically allow one to get rid of one's house phone, PDA and pager (a small electronic device that allowed one to get a brief, non-returnable, one-way message).

 The reason this breakthrough is not immediately attributed to an entrepreneur is, in our case, that it is just as feasible that the research and development department of some business came up with the idea. If the company that manufactured the PDA or the cell phone made components for both, it is just as reasonable to assume that they are the ones that went to their customer and said, "You know, if you want, we could combine the two devices." Whether a businessperson came up with the idea or an entrepreneur is not important, the point is that innovation is not automatically entrepreneurship. It depends on who finds the opportunity and how they go about exploiting it.

Another issue with innovation is, even when it is entrepreneurship, it may only offer the entrepreneur above average profits for a very limited time. This is because protection for most innovation is not available. In our example, electronic phone books, calendars, and calculators already existed and it is extremely difficult to patent or copyright a unique combination of existing items. For this reason, the entrepreneur can expect above average profits only for as long as it takes their competitors to replicate what they have done.

In Chapter 2, we had a brief discussion of the difference between incremental innovation (small changes) and radical innovation (game changers). We can put these two concepts into better perspective using our current discussion of innovation. The combination of the cell phone and the PDA is a radical innovation. This is because such innovation forces the entire market to change the way they do things or perish. Moreover, for as long as it takes the competition to catch up, the innovator (whether entrepreneur or existing business) can make above average profits.

Incremental innovation is in essence, simply an improvement to an existing product, process, or service. The example we used here is the improvement of the cell phone's calendar, calculator, and contact lists. The reason this is virtually never entrepreneurship is that most of these small improvements are simply a selling point designed to keep the existing company competitive. This type of innovation does not provide above average profits, it simply maintains or temporarily increases sales. As a result, this form of innovation is rarely entrepreneurship. Based on these distinctions, it is apparent why we previously stated that innovation is only sometimes entrepreneurship. That is because most of the time radical innovation is entrepreneurship and incremental is not.

Whether you are talking about creativity or innovation, ultimately both really stem from a combination of imagination and inspiration. This type of thinking can take several different forms, all of which, from an entrepreneur's perspective, work to locate or create solutions to problems and ultimately entrepreneurial opportunities. Consequently, in order to help better understand how one becomes creative, it is important that we turn our attention to the different types of creative thinking and how one goes about learning to develop and use these tools in the quest to become an entrepreneur.

Before we start, it is important to understand that creativity is often thought of as a gift that one is blessed with at birth and subsequently a driving force throughout one's life. This is not necessarily true. Almost all of us are born creative. The problem is we have systematically had

Chapter 6: Creativity and Innovation

our creativity stifled as children. Your parents and all the adults in your life did this to you. Their parents did it to them and, I hate to be the one to tell you, but either you are currently or you are going to do it to your children. It happened every time you painted the grass pink in your drawings and people told you that it was wrong. It happened every time you were told you could not do something and were not given a reason why. It happened every time you kept asking questions (but why, but why, but why) and got the answer, "because I said so." Do not blame your parents and try not to blame yourself. It is simply how society sets the rules. By creating what we call social norms, in essence the guidelines we use to know what is and is not acceptable, we learn how to function within our society. The problem is, without knowing why we can or cannot do things we do not always know that what we are doing is the best way of doing it. This is why it is important that as adults, especially ones who wish to become entrepreneurs, we take our creativity back. As we talk about the following methods of thinking creatively, one of the common threads you are going to understand better is just how your creativity has been stifled by those around you and from this understanding just how to become creative once again.

What Psychological Techniques Can We Use to Restart Our Creativity?

Before we head too far down this road, it is important to discuss how to know when someone is attempting to suppress your creativity. As previously mentioned, far too often in our lives, we allow others to suppress our creativity. This eventually leads most of us to stop being creative all together. I do it, you do it, and virtually everyone else does it too. We do it without even realizing we are doing it. We suppress the creativity of others virtually every time someone suggests, or tries to do, something different from what we consider the norm and we say *no*. How do we know we are doing it? Simple, next time someone suggests something that diverges from the norm, before you say no, ask yourself *why* you are about to say no. If your answer is because it has always been done that way or we tried that before and it does not work (provided the attempt was not yesterday), you are suppressing their creativity. Why do we do it? Again, the answer is simple. Overall people do not like change. We are most comfortable when we do things the very same way over and over. We do not have to learn anything new and there is no chance that we may fail because we know we can do it the current way.

The best way to know when your creativity is being suppressed is to then ask *"Why?"* The rule of thumb I use is if you have an idea and someone tells you "no it won't work," "no because it's always been done that way," or something similar, just ask why and keep asking why until they no longer have a good answer, or they give up. Just so you know, most of the time people who do not really know why they are saying no will get frustrated after the second or third why and respond with, "because I said so" or something similarly dismissive. If this person is your current boss, it is time to walk away before you get into trouble. In my experience, if you ask why five times and do not get a good answer every time it is best to pursue your idea or suggestion, even if you have to do it on your own time. This is because chances are good that you have a potential entrepreneurial opportunity. If, however, they are able to give you five good answers, they are probably right and it is time to thank them for their time and let it go.

Now that you know how to spot when someone is trying to suppress you creativity, let us discuss the different ways of thinking that you can use to restart your creativity.

Counterfactual thinking[1] is the process of creating possible alternatives to actual events. Such creativity works primarily through the process of asking oneself *"what if?"* The process forces you to use your imagination to consider possible alternative actions, products, or services that could have led to a different, more favorable outcome. In entrepreneurship, counterfactual thinking is often used to take unwelcome or traumatic events and turn these adversities into opportunities. Often by simply looking at the event and asking oneself, "How could this have been prevented?" an entrepreneur will create potential new products, processes, or services that will help to prevent or alter the outcome of similar events in the future.

One of the best ways to begin thinking creatively is to try to think like a child. A child is learning everything for the first time and, as those of us who have had or been around young kids know, they use counterfactual thinking all the time. Counterfactual thinking is a way of learning what to do and not to do for ourselves. A good example is learning that touching something hot hurts. If a child walks into the kitchen and sees a batch of cookies sitting on the counter they will often simply grab one. After all, if they are sitting out, it must be ok, right? The problem is they did not know the cookies were fresh out of the oven and

---

[1] Markman, K., Klein, W., & Suhr, J. (eds.) (2009). *Handbook of Imagination and Mental Simulation.* New York: Psychology Press

they are still hot. If they really want a cookie (because cookies taste good and they were never hot before) they instinctively use counterfactual thinking to try to solve the problem. They think, "How could I have gotten the cookie and not gotten hurt? I could have waited until it cools, or I could try eating it without using my hands (of course then they will burn their lips and the process will start all over again, trust me I have seen it), or I could ask mom when can I have a cookie." The point is that children often do not simply accept the outcome of a given event. They look at alternatives, even seemingly crazy ones, to find an alternate means of getting what they want without the negative consequences. This is also what entrepreneurs do. Now we could go on and on using children to help us better understand how to begin using counterfactual thinking, but not everyone has had enough exposure to young children to understand what we mean, so let us try an entrepreneurial example.

Ever since the first cars were mass-produced, car thieves have been stealing them. Using counterfactual thinking, in the 1920s the first car alarm was created in an attempt to prevent this from happening. How do we know that counterfactual thinking was used? Simple, there is no reason for one to think about creating such a device, unless they were aware that cars were being stolen. Although there are no records of who created this first device, it must have happened because either the creator's car was stolen, or because it happened to someone the creator knew, or because the creator learned of it from the paper or radio (remember there was no such thing as television or internet at the time). The key is, the creator looked at the problem as a possible opportunity and did so by reflectively looking at how the theft of a car might have been prevented. This is the creative value of counterfactual thinking. However, not every opportunity comes from adversity and thus counterfactual thinking is not the only tool entrepreneurs use to create entrepreneurial opportunities.

Chapter 6: Creativity and Innovation

Divergent thinking[2] is the process of generating creative ideas or solutions by taking knowledge from other, seemingly unrelated, areas and applying it to a problem at hand. This method tends to generate many possible ideas or solutions in a short period, like brainstorming, with unexpected connections the goal. Once all possible ideas or solutions are exhausted, each is then evaluated to determine the best possible idea or solution to the problem. Entrepreneurs often use this method to overcome obstacles that others deem impossible.

For example, a certain entrepreneur has knowledge of all kinds of entrepreneurial behavior (good and bad), and knowledge of manufacturing, computers, teaching, repairing old houses, working in restaurants, the workings of universities, how to edit (video and audio) computer and internet programs, and is a non-traditional student from age 38 to 50. From this varied knowledge several potential entrepreneurial opportunities have come.

1. *This book*—real knowledge of what entrepreneurship is and is not, what entrepreneurs do, and what you can do to become an entrepreneur *(Entrepreneurial Behavior + Teaching + Manufacturing + Non-Traditional Student + Computers and Computer Programs)*.

2. *Electronic classroom*—a electronic classroom that works the exact same way as a traditional classroom except fully online, including being able to see, hear, and interact with your instructor and all your fellow classmates no matter where they are, and allowing a person to take a class from a specific professor. No matter who or where you are or even what school you attend *(Entrepreneurship + Computers +*

---

[2] Guilford, J.P. (1967). *The Nature of Human Intelligence.* New York: McGraw-Hill

Teaching + Non-Traditional Student + Computer and Internet Programs such as Adobe Creative Suite™, Skype™, YouTube™, Blackboard™ + Restaurants and Manufacturing [customer service, i.e., giving the customers what they want, not what you want to give them]).

3. *Course in an eBook*—everything you get from a classroom in an eBook, including text, lectures with PowerPoint™ slides, video clips, assignments, exams, additional optional materials, and frequently asked questions *(Entrepreneurship + Computers + Teaching + Non-Traditional Student + Computer and Internet Programs such as Adobe Creative Suite™, Skype™, YouTube™, Blackboard™ + Restaurants and Manufacturing [customer service]).*

Moreover, these are but three of the entrepreneurial opportunities that have come from the use of divergent thinking with the varied knowledge and experience listed above. I can assure you, there are many more and I assure you several are quite out there. Another similar, yet different method of creative thinking is conceptual blending.

Conceptual blending[3,4] is the result of two quite different things being brought together to create something completely new and unique. For the entrepreneur, this means taking two or more areas of which they have knowledge and attempting to combine them. Let us see how that might work. Say an entrepreneur has extensive knowledge of

---

[3] Koestler, A. (1964). *The Act of Creation.* London: Pan Books
[4] Turner, M., & Fauconnier, G. (2002). *The Way We Think. Conceptual Blending and the Mind's Hidden Complexities.* New York: Basic Books

Chapter 6: Creativity and Innovation

rock climbing and skydiving. Although these two areas may seem to have little in common, the unique knowledge of each could yield new products, processes, or services. For example:

- *Personal hover pack* (for people who wish to see the rock climbing view but cannot climb—not all ideas have to be reasonable, sometimes they lead to other things)
- *Autochute* (parachute for when free climbers fall)
- *Very low level parachutes* (for use with the Autochute)
- *Climber counterweight* (for use with beginning climbers, if you fall you land safely—uses the same type of harness as a parachute)
- *Video recording of your climb* (uses a remote control helicopter with video camera)
- *Personal Airbag* (for when your chute does not open or climbers fall)

Additionally, ideas may lead to products, processes, or services that can be used in other markets. For example, the Autochute and the Personal Airbag are both items that can be marketed to companies and people who work or live in skyscrapers. The conceptual blending of multiple areas of knowledge and experience can bring the inspiration needed to create new and unique entrepreneurial opportunities. Now that you understand some of the important psychological techniques useful in the reawakening of your creative side, it is time to look at some of the other things that creative people do to help get their creative juices flowing.

Additional Tips to Help Improve One's Creativity

Make Time

One of the biggest problems in today's society is that people just do not make the time to come to a complete stop and just think. With all the hustle and bustle of modern life, between work and a social life, and responsibilities to our family, friends, and children, we just never find the time to stop and just let our minds wander. This is where creativity lives. The mind is an

100   *Discovering the Entrepreneur Within*

amazing thing—it thrives on constant input. In today's society, it is not hard for our minds to find all the input they can handle. Most of us do not even realize the full extent of the massive amount of input our minds are receiving. Let me give you an example.

My two youngest children (14 and 16) come home every day from school and go straight to their rooms to do their homework (it is the rule at our house). However, walk in on them and what you see is typical of the over stimulation of the mind we have been talking about. They are doing their homework, listening to the television or radio, texting, and watching YouTube™ videos, all at the same time. Only if the homework is extremely hard do they turn off one or two of the inputs (never all of them) and, believe it or not, they always get really good grades. The point is if you are having a hard time being creative, often it is because you need to make time to do nothing but be creative.

Find a Quiet Space

This can be extremely helpful for the creative process. Even when we turn off our radios, televisions, and cell phones, we often realize that the space we are in is still full of useless input like other people talking, their devices making noise, dogs barking, etc. This is why it is important to find a quiet space free of virtually all distractions. For me I go for a long drive (without the radio and cell phone on) or go out, sit in the woods, or send everyone out to the movies and go into my office. Once you have made the time and found a space, now you simply need to let your mind wander.

Chapter 6: Creativity and Innovation

Free Your Mind

As mentioned, our brains crave constant input. The great thing is that if you deprive your brain of external input, it will eventually create its own input by daydreaming. Once you start, it is normal for your mind to focus on things that are important to you, what you need to do for the day, what you are going to do after you finish thinking, and anything else that has been on your mind. That is ok and actually part of the creative process. If there is anything bothering you, you will need to resolve it or realize you cannot resolve it at this time, before your mind will let go and move on to other things. Only when these things have been resolved or reviewed will your mind begin to wander. In fact, these issues may even be the beginning of the creative process by looking for ways of solving these problems. This leads us to a discussion of how you can steer your mind into a specific direction.

Once you have freed your mind of all the external and internal noise or distractions, it is possible to focus it in the direction you want it to go. You do this by focusing on the problem you wish to solve, or on areas you wish to locate an opportunity, and just let your mind go. You will come up with some crazy ideas. That is normal. Do not ignore anything. Everything, no matter how out there, may have real entrepreneurial potential once the idea is refined later. It is important to understand that this is not something you do every once in a while when you need an idea or to solve a problem. Freeing your mind to be creative is something you need to do on a regular basis. It does not have to be daily (although you will get the best results if you can) but you need to do this at least once a week to get the full benefits. Creativity comes in its own time. All you can do is to create a regular time where you open the door for your creativity to come in.

Another thing to note is that your mind needs to be free of chemical influences. I cannot tell you how many people I have known who claim that their creativity is heightened when they use illegal substances or alcohol. This is bull. Do not get me wrong, I am neither against nor in favor of the personal use of such substances, I believe if you are not hurting anyone else then it is not for me to judge. Nevertheless, the mind is a machine and it runs best when it is finely tuned and free of anything that alters its normal function. Just imagine what these people could create if their minds were clear.

Sleep Can be Your Friend

Throughout the day, our minds take in far more information than they can process. We store this information for processing later. Most often, this takes place when we sleep. Dreams are often just our minds processing the day's information, determining what to save and what to discard. The mind really is an amazing thing. It not only looks at the pieces of information it has gathered throughout the day individually to determine usefulness, it also looks for unexpected connections between pieces of information using all of the techniques we discussed earlier (counterfactual thinking, divergent thinking, and conceptual blending). These manifest as nightmares (counterfactual thinking) and strange dreams (divergent thinking and conceptual blending). This is why we often go to sleep with problems we cannot solve and wake up with the answers to these problems. Based on this knowledge, it is possible to guide your mind to work on certain problems while you sleep. Now, this does not always work. If your mind deems something else is more important it will work on that first, but if you focus on the problem you wish to solve just before going to sleep, the chance of waking up with the solution is increased.

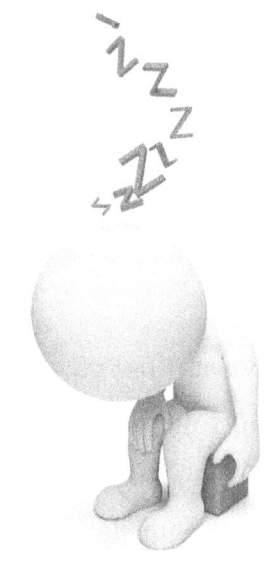

If you are having trouble believing this concept, take a moment and think about it. How many times have you watched a movie right before bed and your dreams seem to focus on the movie? Maybe you dream you are in the movie or maybe a character from the movie seems to be in your everyday life. This is how you know the sleeping mind can be focused.

Write It Down

Once the mind solves a problem or comes up with an idea, it has a tendency to forget it. I cannot tell you how many times I have woken up with, or came up with during the day, a great idea or solution to a problem only to lose it. At the time, the idea or solution was so great that I thought there was no way I could ever forget it. Trust me when I tell you, you will forget so write it down immediately. Do not wait. I do not care if you have to interrupt an important phone call, get up in the middle of the night, or stop right in the middle of doing anything (yes, anything). Because I can assure you that once that idea or solution is gone, it is gone forever and you will kick yourself. I have done it a hundred times and so has most everyone I have known. I use my cell phone. Most cell phones come with a recording application. If yours did not, I cannot suggest strongly enough that you get one. It will save your sanity.

Eventually, we all get to a point where we are no longer able to be creative on our own. Everything that used to work no longer seems to be working. Here are two things you can do to help regain your creative momentum.

Be Observant

If you have no problems and ideas seem to be few and far in between, one way to regain your creative momentum is by observing others. As you go through your day, watch and listen to those around you. You will be surprised how often people will give you fuel for your creative engine. For example, every time you hear someone say, "I wish," "I want," "I need," or "I hate" there is a problem that your creativity may be able to solve. Whenever you see someone dealing with a problem, again you are seeing a problem that your creativity may be able to solve.

Learn Something New Every Day

Another thing you can do to keep your creative juices flowing is to learn. As we have seen, creative techniques often require taking things that do not normally go together and trying to find a way to put them together. Therefore, the more you know, the more you have to work with. Now this is not limited to formal learning (taking classes or reading books) it applies equally to anything you do not currently know (swimming, skydiving, knitting, cooking, etc.). All learning adds to your creative ability.

The Last Thing You Need to Know About Creativity

Creativity is a wonderful thing. However, it is possible, when we are on our own, to convince ourselves that almost anything is a great idea or a great solution to a problem. Unfortunately, a good example of this is suicide. ***Please*** do not think me cold or uncaring, but in too many cases, it is a permanent solution to a temporary problem. This is why it is so important to find someone to bounce your ideas, and solutions to problems, off. It is the only way to ensure that you are making the right choices in life. This person can be anyone, family, friend, acquaintance, professional, even a stranger who will listen. The key is we all need someone to make sure that our creativity does not go too far.

Chapter 7:

Psychological Hardiness and the Entrepreneur

In Chapter 5 we discussed what it takes to create an entrepreneurial mindset. One of the concepts not mentioned was that of psychological hardiness. Although not necessarily a direct factor in the mindset formation process, it is a significant factor in the everyday life of an entrepreneur and as such is the topic of this chapter.

Psychological Hardiness

Uncertainty and risk accompany entrepreneurs throughout the entire entrepreneurial process. The strength of one's belief in one's ability to learn whatever one needs to know along the way, *dynamic entity schema* and *intellectual self*, and the belief in one's ability to create a given outcome, *self-efficacy*, are some of the driving forces that keep an entrepreneur moving forward throughout the process. Still the inevitable failures, obstacles, stressors, and occasional self-doubt associated with the entrepreneurial process are enough to shake anyone's beliefs. One of the factors that keep entrepreneurs moving forward when this happens is psychological hardiness.[1] **Psychological hardiness** is one's emotional propensity to stand in defiance of challenges and mentally recover from failure.[2] In essence, psychological hardiness is what entrepreneurs use to survive emotionally, and even thrive, when their beliefs in themselves or their decisions are tested.

How Does Psychological Hardiness Work?

Generally, people high in psychological hardiness have a strong sense of *commitment* to life and work, are actively engaged in what is going on around them, and believe they can *control* or influence what happens to them. Such individuals enjoy new situations and challenges. They are internally motivated, tend to create

---

[1] Sinclair and D'Souza, in progress
[2] Kobasa, S.C., Maddi, S.R., & Kahn, S. (1982). Hardiness and health: A prospective study. *Journal of Personality and Social Psychology* 42: 168-177.

their own sense of purpose, and see change as an exciting *challenge*.[3] When applied to entrepreneurs, it is easy to see that many of the same qualities that work to form an entrepreneurial mindset also work to make a person psychologically hardy. This is not to say that all entrepreneurs are psychologically hardy or that all psychologically hardy individuals are, or should be, entrepreneurs. Just that those psychologically hardy entrepreneurs seem to have a greater mental ability to survive, and thrive, the entrepreneurial process.

Commitment, as it pertains to psychological hardiness, is a person's ability to believe in the value of who they are, self-concept, and what they are doing, like entrepreneurial behavior. Such *self-confidence* causes people to involve themselves fully in entrepreneurial behavior. Researchers have shown that the tendency to commit fully is one of the factors that allow a person to ward off the illness-provoking effects of stress.[3] Such a commitment to oneself provides an overall sense of purpose that eases the stress of any given perceived threat related to entrepreneurial behavior, even when the stressful behavior is a threat to one's view of oneself[3] (e.g., a failed attempt to start an entrepreneurial venture). Such commitment

---

[3] Kobasa, S. (1979). Stressful life events, personality, and health: An inquiry into hardiness. *Journal of Personality and Social Psychology* **37**(1): 1-11.

serves as a buffer between the threat and one's perception of oneself. Committed people know not only *what* they are involved in when choosing entrepreneurial behavior (knowledge), but also *why* they chose to be involved in entrepreneurial behavior (motivation). A stressful event like failure may counteract one's confidence in what they believe entrepreneurial behavior is (their knowledge), but not why they chose to become an entrepreneur (their motivation).

For true commitment to exist, one must first identify one's distinctive goals and priorities, and possess the confidence in one's ability to make decisions and the ability to hold true to one's values. This kind of self-confidence supports and renews the internal structure and strength that researchers deem essential for the accurate assessment and competent handling of any life situation,[4] like entrepreneurial behavior. However, commitment requires more than a strong sense of self-confidence. It also requires a sense of accountability to others. This sense of accountability benefits a person's commitment by affording them the knowledge that in times of stress, or great need, there are people they can turn to—*support*. With commitment also comes a sense of *responsibility* that others are counting on one not to give up in times of great difficulty and pressure. This sense of accountability is one of the most fundamental resources for successfully coping with stress.[5]

In short, committed persons have both the skill and desire to cope successfully with stress because 1) they have confidence in their decision making ability and their ability to hold true to their values, which in turn creates a sense of value in who they

---

[4] White, R. W. (1959). Motivation reconsidered: The concept of competence. *Psychological Review* 66(5): 297-333

[5] Antonovsky, A. (1979). *Health, Stress, and Coping.* John Wiley & Sons, San Francisco.

are—*self-confidence*. 2) They have the ability to set distinctive goals that allow them to see the true value in what they are doing—*knowledge*. 3) They feel *support* from, and a *responsibility* to, those who are relying on them to complete what they have started—*motivation*. However, commitment is but one of the factors necessary for the development of a psychologically hardy individual. Another of these factors is control.

Control is one's tendency to believe and act as if one can influence the course of events—*self-efficacy*. People who feel they are in control see explanations for why something is happening. They tend not to blame others for problems, or fate, but instead focus on their own responsibility for the given situation—*internal locus of control*. This efficacy of control works to ward off the harmful physical effect of stress.[6] Such control allows a person to perceive many stressful life events as predictable consequences of their own activity and thus subject to their direction and manipulation. Persons with a strong efficacy of control recognize their role in all that happens to them, even when others may not. For example, an entrepreneur closes a venture due to poor performance in a time of great economic distress in the area. Although most everyone would state that the fault of the failure lies in the economy and not with the entrepreneur, those entrepreneurs with a strong efficacy of control recognize their role in the failure. Not as a source of blame, but as a learning experience; specifically, what could they have done differently (e.g., waited to start the venture, downsized sooner, move the venture to a different area, etc.).

---

[6] Bandura, A. (1986). *Social Foundations of Thought and Action: A Social Cognitive Theory.* Englewood Cliffs, New Jersey, Prentice-Hall.

Even when entrepreneurs believe there was nothing they could have done (e.g., the death of a loved one), they tend to confront the event in the spirit of control. Not necessarily what they could have done to prevent it (although many opportunities have come about this way), but what can they learn from it (e.g., take better care of themselves, spend more time with loved ones, etc.). From this, we can see that psychologically hardy individuals tend to have a variety of effective responses to stressful life events including cognitive, decisional, and behavioral dimensions of control.[7] However, before we continue, it is important to point out that it is the perception of control, not the accuracy of that perception, which affects stress. Additionally, the effects of the three types of control are not additive. In fact, researchers have shown that the three work in complex ways with any one type enhancing, nullifying, or even reversing the effects of another depending on the circumstances.[8] At this point, it is time to discuss each of the three types of control as they specifically pertain to entrepreneurship.

Cognitive control refers to how a person interprets, appraises, and incorporates stressful events into one's life in such a way as to reduce the effects of stress through continuous exposure.[3] In entrepreneurship this relates to one's belief in one's ability to detect warning signals early enough to react either decisionally or behaviorally. Such a perception of vision reduces stress by lowering one's fear of the unknown.

Think of cognitive control as driving a car. If one is driving at night, in a completely unfamiliar rural area, one's stress level is bound to

---

[7] Averill, J.R. (1973). Personal control over aversive stimuli and its relationship to stress. *Psychological Bulletin* 80(4): 286-303.
[8] Veitch, J.A. & Gifford, R. (1996). Choice, perceived control, and performance in physical environments. *Journal of Environmental Psychology* 16: 269-276.

be quite high. This is because it is unfamiliar territory, the driver has no idea what lies ahead, is not used to driving at night, and has a limited line of sight. Now instead of attempting to avoid such situations as most people might, metaphorically, psychologically hardy people would drive under these conditions as often as possible. They will do so in order to gain the confidence that even though they are extremely limited in their ability see what is up ahead, and they are not familiar with an area, they are certain they can handle whatever might jump out at them (a sharp turn or a deer). This is because eventually they will have experienced such events and therefore believe they can handle them or any other unexpected events like them. Such exposure to things we are afraid of increases our confidence and in turn reduces our stress related to such activities by giving us the ability to *interpret* what is likely to happen, and quickly *appraise* a situation as it is happening by *incorporating* similar situations in our everyday life on a regular basis.

For potential entrepreneurs and entrepreneurs alike, this means regular exposure to events that require quick decision making and problem solving skills, thus reducing the stressful effect of uncertainty that accompanies the entrepreneurial process.

Decisional control, as it relates to psychological hardiness and stress, refers to one's ability to hold multiple alternative options to achieving a given goal.[3] Thus, stress is reduced as alternative decisions exist that allow one the option to change paths mid-stream should failure of the current path appear to be imminent. However, uncertainty as to the success potential of such alternatives can act to compromise the stress reducing ability of decisional control.[9] In essence, what we are saying is that the more options one has for achieving a desired outcome, for example having a career that gives one a reasonable degree of financial comfort, the less stressful the process. That is, provided that knowledge of truly viable alternate options exists.

A good example of decisional control is career choice. Although a person may have chosen to become an entrepreneur, the knowledge that one is also qualified for other, reasonably satisfying, careers allows for the reduction of stress relating to the choice of an entrepreneurial career. This is because the person knows that, should it be necessary, additional career options exist, such as working in management for an existing company, running a company for someone else, or even teaching entrepreneurship (should the person be so educated).

Behavioral control is one's perception of having at one's disposal a behavioral response that can prevent, reduce, or terminate stressful situations.[3] Thus, stress is reduced by the degree that perceived alternative behavioral options are seen to exist. Belief in these alternative behavioral options is dependent on the perceived resources and opportunities available to the individual (i.e., knowledge of entrepreneurship, skill and abilities related to entrepreneurial behavior, etc.), and the greater the perceived number of alternatives the greater the perception of behavioral control.[10]

---

[9] Shanahan, M.J., & Neufeld, R.W.J. (2010). Coping with stress through decisional control: Quantification of negotiating the environment. *British Journal of Mathematical and Statistical Psychology*, 63, 575-601.

[10] Ajzen, I. (1985). From intentions to actions: A theory of planned behavior. In: J. Kuhl and J. Beckman (Eds.) *Action-Control: From Cognition to Behavior.* Heidelberg: Springer, 11-39.

Based in part on experience with a given behavior, or behavior that is perceived as similar, such perceptions of behavioral control are built. However, behavioral control may also be influenced by second-hand information about the behavior, such as through experiences shared by friends, family, and acquaintances, and by other factors that increase or reduce the perceived difficulty of performing the behavior in question.[11]

Let us look at an example. If you choose to become an entrepreneur by starting an entrepreneurial venture, you will experience a greater degree of stress if the only way you know how to become an entrepreneur is by starting an entrepreneurial venture. However, if the goal is to become an entrepreneur, not just to start a business, then the knowledge of the different pathways to becoming an entrepreneur reduces the stress related to the entrepreneurial process. This is because, although you plan to

---

[11] Ajzen, I., & Madden, T.J. (1986). Prediction of goal-directed behavior: Attitudes, intentions, and perceived behavioral control. *Journal of Experimental Social Psychology* 22: 453-474.

start an entrepreneurial venture, you know that if it appears that the venture may not be right for you, you have alternative entrepreneurial (behavioral) options to fall back on. For example, partner with someone with the knowledge you are lacking, sell the idea to an existing company or a nascent entrepreneur looking for a business opportunity, and so forth. These known and viable alternatives reduce the stress of becoming an entrepreneur. However, these alternatives only act to reduce stress if the individual is aware of them and how to go about utilizing them should the need arise.

Challenge, in reference to psychological hardiness, is the belief that change rather than stability is a normal way of life. From this perspective, change is an opportunity and incentive for personal growth, rather than a threat to security. When change is seen as a good thing, much of the disruption associated with change can be anticipated, thus reducing the stress of any given life event. Viewing change as a challenge leads people to become the catalyst of change in their own environments and to practice responding to the unexpected. Because of a fondness for change, such individuals search for more and interesting experiences. This is not to say that such persons are reckless or irresponsible; on the contrary, psychologically hardy people search for novelty as a means of continually improving their lives, not putting them at risk or seeking an adrenaline rush. Persons who welcome the challenge of change know where to turn to for help in coping with stress. Further, such people hold an openness, or cognitive flexibility, toward ambiguity and uncertainty. This allows them to integrate and appraise effectively the threat of even the most unexpected stressful life events.[3] This view of change as a challenge also leads them to be motivated to persist even when new information is contradictory to their initial beliefs.[12]

As previously stated, entrepreneurship is not automatically a permanent state. As a result, true entrepreneurs tend to be continually looking for new and better entrepreneurial opportunities. This view of change as a way of life, and their fondness for the challenge of new and more interesting experiences, is one of the things that tend to make entrepreneurs psychologically hardy individuals.

As you can see, there are both similarities and differences among the three components of psychological hardiness (*commitment*, *control*, and *challenge*). When viewed as interactive parts of an overall style, these components lead to a resistance to stress that decreases the number and severity of illnesses. Now it is important to understand that being psychologically hardy does not mean one is immune to all forms of illness. Although psychological hardiness does help one prevent common illnesses, such as the common cold and the flu, it does not affect one's ability to ward off illness that one is genetically predisposed to (e.g., cancer, heart conditions, etc.). However, being psychologically hardy does help one recover from these types of illness better and faster than those who are not psychologically hardy.

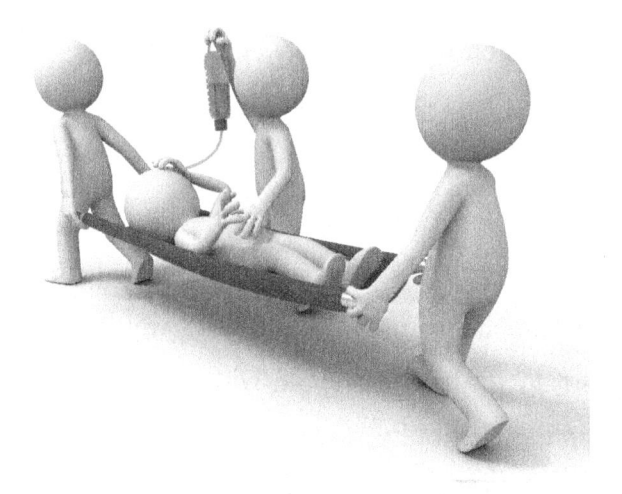

---

[12] Moss, G. E. (1973). *Illness, Immunity, and Social Interaction.* New York: Wiley Publishing.

Chapter 8:

Ethics and the Entrepreneur

Now that we have covered the basics of what makes one an entrepreneur, it is now necessary to discuss the ethical implications of such a choice.

What Are Ethics?

The meaning of the word ethics can be hard to pin down. The reason is that ethics means different things to different groups. For example, an action that is ethical to one group can easily be unethical to another (e.g., soldiers and pacifists). Furthermore, people who are members of multiple groups may find themselves in a situation in which they follow one set of ethical rules in one part of their life and a contradictory set of ethical rules in another (e.g., religion and job). To help to minimize such confusion, we will first specifically define ethics.

The Merriam-Webster dictionary defines ethics as "rules of behavior based on ideas about what is morally good and bad." In this definition, it would seem that ethics are in essence one's morals. This then bares the question, what then are morals? Merriam-Webster goes on to define morals as "based on what you think is right and good." Thus, based on these two definitions a simple explanation of ethics would be that **ethics** are a set of rules in regards to how one should behave based on what they believe is right and wrong. We will use this definition in our discussion of ethics.

The Need for Ethics in Entrepreneurship

One might say, "I am a good person, I don't need a lesson on ethics." and in general this may be very true. Entrepreneurship, however, poses a unique set of circumstances, which, if left unchecked, can cause us to deviate drastically from who we are in our everyday lives. Let me explain. Few entrepreneurs start out with the intent of undertaking unethical behavior. Most often, such choices in my experience are traceable back to one of two situations. The entrepreneur *felt they had no choice*, or it was something that, over time, the entrepreneur worked their way into (often without really realizing it). In our context, this can be described quite simply with the statement "... absolute power corrupts absolutely."[1] Now these statements may seem to many to be nothing more than excuses, and with that, I will not argue. What is more important is that both situations are avoidable. Before we discuss methods for avoiding such situations, it is important to look at how each can occur.

"I Had No Choice"

Unlike other professions in which people find themselves in positions that hold significant power over the lives of others (doctors, lawyers, psychologists, etc.) entrepreneurship has no formal code of ethics. A **code of ethics** is a set of rules adopted (often formally) by a group whose actions can put individuals within their care at risk. Although entrepreneurship may not be in the same league as the professions previously mentioned, when it comes to the damage these professionals can cause to a person under their care, it is important to remember that in the beginning of virtually all entrepreneurial ventures the entrepreneur must persuade others to take a chance on them. As we have seen, the people they are most able to convince are those who are closest to them (family and friends) and those who are in desperate need of what they are offering (a steady income, security, possibly insurance, a chance to better their life, etc). Because such people are relying on the entrepreneur to protect them from harm, and as we

---

[1] Acton, J.E.E.D. (1887), in a letter to Bishop Mandell Creighton.

Chapter 8: Ethics and the Entrepreneur

have learned in an earlier chapter the entrepreneur cares for these people, an entrepreneur is at risk for acting unethically in situations that may cause harm to those they feel are in their care (family, friends, employees, etc). Let us look at an example where entrepreneurs may find themselves in just such a situation.

Assume that you have started a business and you are just starting to do quite well. The people you have persuaded to invest in you and come to work for you are finally starting to breathe a sigh of relief. Believing that all the risk they have taken and the fear they felt is finally behind them. You did everything you said you would and to these people you are somewhat of a hero. You wake up every day feeling vindicated in the eyes of all those who told you that you would never pull it off, or were not smart enough, or any of the other million things you where told along the way all intended to prevent you from trying to become an entrepreneur. At this moment, you are on top of the world.

Now let us add an all too possible situation into the mix, one that I hope you never come across in real life. A new customer of yours has decided to place a huge order ($500,000 for tooling and $500,000 worth of parts in the first year, $1,000,000 total). One bigger than anything you have ever received before (up until this point your yearly sales were only $750,000). Your company is capable of producing the order, although you will have to use every drop of credit you have available to you and then some, but that is ok because this order will take you to the next level, a level that truly offers everyone who put faith in you permanent protection against harm. Even though you know the customer is upstanding, because you have checked every reference they gave you, checked with the better business bureau and found they have a top rating, you have an attorney draw up a contract further insuring payment. With all this in hand, you prepare to fill the order.

The first order of business is buying the tools you need to produce such a large order ($450,000, yes you make profit off the tooling too). Next, you order the raw materials to produce the products from the tooling ($50,000). Then you pay employees to set up the tooling, test to make sure the tooling works properly, run preliminary samples, and certify the quality before you send them to the customer for approval ($7,500). To this point, you have invested $507,500 in the project and have invoiced the customer $500,000 for the tooling upon approval of samples (due within 30 days) with the other $7,500 coming out of the profits you make from your other customers. Now all you have to do is wait to be paid. Both the tooling manufacturer and the raw materials company have given you 90 days (3 months) to pay them. At this point, these companies know they can trust you and it does not hurt that you are about to be an even bigger customer of theirs. Now it is just a waiting game.

One month later, almost to the day, you receive approval for your parts but no check. You contact the customer and find that their customer (a company in Germany) is thrilled with the parts you produced. The problem is your customer is waiting for payment from their customer. They tell you it should only be a few days—two weeks tops (can you see where this is going). After two weeks, even more excuses. A few more weeks and they stop taking your calls (everyone is always in meetings). Finally, you are almost out of time so you have the attorney who drew up the contract contact them. That will do the trick. After all, you have an ironclad contract—right?

A few days later, you receive a call from the attorney. It turns out that your customer placed the order on speculation. **Speculation** occurs when a company takes it upon themselves to take the risk that a gamble will pay off. In this case, your customer placed the order with you expecting that their "potential" customer, once they see how well and inexpensive you could make the parts, would stop using their current supplier and start buying the parts from your customer (in essence you). In short they were gambling (something entrepreneurs do not do) that they could get the company in Germany to buy from them. The good news is you do in fact have an ironclad contract and, if you decide to sue, the attorney assures you that you will win without a doubt. The bad news is it will cost your company $50,000 to win and you will actually never see a penny from your former customer. Why—it turns out that while you were waiting for them to pay you, they were in fact starting a new company in another country and managed to sell every single asset to that company for $1. Oh, and by the way, the owners moved to that country too. Therefore, your company is now $500,000 in debt and you have three options that I can see.

1. *Struggle and try to get through it.* Try to find a way to get the people you owe to agree to a payment program, if you can. Your company makes about $75,000 total profit (including your salary). Based on this it will take 7 1/2 years ($67,500 and $6,750 respectively), during which you will receive no salary at all for at least five of those years.
2. *File bankruptcy.* Letting all those who trusted in you down, in addition to proving right all those who said you could not or should not be an entrepreneur.

3. *Bend some laws.* Just a little until you get back on your feet (I am not going to tell you how, I do not want to take a chance on someone using such information as a guide to follow this route). After all you did everything right and there is no reason everyone around you should pay for what that dishonest company did (and why should those people who said you could not or should not become an entrepreneur be proven right when in fact they are not right—no one could have prevented this situation from happening).

So what would you do? If you are being honest with yourself, the answer is not very simple is it? Let us assume someone else, not you, chose #3 (you are far too honest to consider ever bending the law). What we have is one company that put themselves in an ethical dilemma by *gambling* and another by using *rationalization*. While these are but two of several ways entrepreneurs can find themselves in an ethical dilemma relating to what I call "I had no choice," the point is that it is possible for the best of us to fall victim to bad choices, if you are not prepared. However, we will talk more about that a little later in the chapter. Unfortunately, even when entrepreneurs are able to avoid such situations, they are still at risk of acting unethically.

"Absolute Power Corrupts Absolutely"

One of the biggest problems facing successful first time entrepreneurs is the risk of letting success go to their heads. Think about it, you have just worked years to make your dream a reality. Many, many people along the way told you that you could not do it, or you did not have what it takes to make it happen, and now you have proven all of them wrong. These people now recognize and acknowledge your skills and abilities as an entrepreneur and it feels great. You are large and in charge and feel like no one can question your decisions ever again, at least when it comes to entrepreneurship. Herein lies the problem, you report to virtually no one. Within your world what you say goes and, to make it worse, most people start agreeing with virtually everything you say and do because they recognize you as the expert.

This is the formula for allowing power to change you. Remember virtually no one starts out acting unethically. It is most often something that one slowly slips into over time. Think of it this way. No one starts out abusing another person, do they? Can you imagine the following situation ever happening? You or someone you know go on a blind date. The person you are meeting walks up and says, "Hello, you are fat and ugly and will never find anyone to love you so you might just as well do what I say, when I say, how I say, and if you do it to my satisfaction I might just love you. You know I am the only person who possibly can." Then they proceed to slap that person and say, "I asked you a question, answer me!" I know this seems a little harsh and you may be asking yourself, "What does this have to do with entrepreneurship?" I ask that you bear with me just a little further.

Virtually no one, even those with the lowest of self-esteem, would tolerate such behavior if it started on day one. Given this, abuse must be something that one slowly learns to accept over time. Inversely, a person who is going to abuse (whether it be another person or abuse of power), must begin by doing so a little at a time, if not they would not get away with it. It is much like the boiling frog syndrome. In case you have not heard the story,[2] it goes like this: If you drop a frog into boiling water, it will jump right back out. This only makes sense. However, if you put the frog in cold water and slowly bring the water to a boil the frog will sit there and boil to death. Now some might say, "This makes sense but only for people who are prone to being

---

[2] Yes, it is but a story. Research has shown that the frog will in fact jump out of the water when it starts to get hot.

abusive." Let us look at another example, maybe this will make it easier to accept the premise that virtually all of us are at risk of letting power go to our heads if we are not careful.

It seems logical that leaders of religious[3] groups, especially well established nationwide groups, must be exempt from such abuses of power. After all, they are men and women of God. I wish that were true. However, experience shows us that is not always the case. These people are mere humans after all and as such subject to all the same risks and temptations as the rest of us. The best example of such human weakness that I know of was all the turmoil that took place in the mid to late 1980s. We had one leader who convinced his people that God wanted them to have a water park. Another religious leader later exposed this same leader for having an affair with his secretary, who himself was then found to be paying women to have relations with him (talk about not throwing stones). Best of all was the religious leader who told his people that if he did not raise an extra $8,000,000 this year,[4] "God said... I will take you home!" By the way, he did not raise all the money and yet lived for another 13 years. I guess God was just kidding. The point is if these mainstream religious leaders (not religious nuts) can end up abusing their power, almost all of us are at risk. I am willing to bet that most, if not all of these people, started out with the best of intentions. It is my experience that what happened was that these leaders simply never thought that it could happen to them. That their ethics were beyond reproach and for that reason they never even considered the possibility that they could

---

[3] This discussion is in no way intended to demean or undermine any religious group. It is strictly intended to expose a potential human weakness in all of us.
[4] *Christianity Today*, February 1987.

Chapter 8: Ethics and the Entrepreneur

end up acting unethically. Therein lays the problem. If you do not know where the line is, how will you know you are about to, or worse already have, crossed the line?

If you have gotten nothing else from the information provided to this point, I hope you can see that no matter who you are, or think you are, you ARE capable of acting unethically, and even illegally, under the right conditions. This is extremely important if you want to be an ethical entrepreneur because if you do not believe you are capable of ever acting unethically, or illegally, you will never see the temptation coming, and believe me it will come. Once you accept the fact that anyone, even you, can act unethically or illegally in certain situations then you can begin to take steps to prevent it from happening to you. We begin by determining where your line is.

Avoiding Ethical Dilemmas

As we have seen, ethical dilemmas tend to sneak up on an entrepreneur. It is rare that they come at you yelling and screaming. Therefore, the only way to prevent such dilemmas is to make sure that you see them coming a mile away, far enough away that you can change your path before they get here. There are several ways to avoid or reduce ethical dilemmas in your entrepreneurial venture and any one of them will work as long as you are honest with yourself and those you trust to help you. The following suggestion is but one of these ways.

Determine your Values

In my experience, the best way to avoid ethical issues is to stay as far away from them as possible. The only way I know how to stay away from such issues is to start by knowing exactly who you are as a person so you know exactly where you are at risk for acting unethically. This means sitting down and determining what exactly your values are. You may say, "I already know exactly what my values are." Good, write them down. I think you will find that you might not be as clear on them as you think you are, at least not specifically. For the rest of us, we need to start with really looking at, not only who we are, but also who we want to be. For example, you might say, "I want to make the world a better place." Ok, how exactly? You have to be specific. Do you want to end world hunger, environmental abuse, discrimination, child abuse, etc.? These are all great causes but you are only one person and you can only do so much no matter how rich you might become.

I suggest starting with what it is you truly believe in (not the things that you feel you should believe in). For example, start with the things you would literally give your life for and move on from there. For example, you might say, "I would give my life to protect my children from harm." Because of this, one of your core values or beliefs must be that parents should be willing to sacrifice anything to care for and protect their children. Remember, this has nothing to do with what people think of you. You know it is truly valid if you would feel this way even if no one ever knows. That in my opinion is the true test of a core value.

Some may have values that they feel are, let us call them, less than honorable (e.g., my happiness is all that matters in life). That is fine. At least you are being honest with yourself. Remember, this book is not about judgment; it is about knowledge. However, if your happiness is your only core value this chapter is not going to do you much good. Even so, I encourage you to continue, you may change how you feel later, for example, once you have kids and if so this information will come in handy. Core values should not be frivolous or unachievable, such as, I want to make the whole world happy or world peace—we all want that. They should be limited to those things that matter most to you that you can actually affect. For example, let us say someone's core values are:

1. Do whatever it takes to protect your kids from harm (and I do mean whatever it takes).
2. Do everything you can to be happy, you only live once (unless you believe in reincarnation).
3. Do not expect others to make you happy, it is not their job.
4. Treat others as you would want to be treated.
5. Do everything you can to protect those who cannot protect themselves.
6. Do everything you can to make those who care about you proud.

Once you have determined your core beliefs, you now know what exactly can cause you to abandon or modify your ethics. This is because your core beliefs are the things that you believe to be more important than any ethics, morals, or laws set down by others. For example, based on the core beliefs above, people will, without a doubt, act unethically to protect their kids from harm if they feel there is no other choice. Based on core belief #1 they are willing to lie, cheat, steal, and if necessary, even commit murder to protect their kids. They are also willing to act unethically in order to help others who cannot protect themselves, provided it will not put their kids at risk or make those they care about ashamed (based on #5, #4, #1, and #6 respectively). Additionally, they are willing to act unethically in order to be happy, provided it will not hurt others or make those who care about them ashamed (based on #2, #3, #4, #5, and #6). All of these appear to be honorable reasons for crossing the ethical line. The problem is, the first time you cross that line it is hard. Every time after that it gets easier and easier. Additionally, the more you cross the line, and get away with it, the more reasons you will find for doing it because it gets to be exciting. Let us take a crazy example to make sure the point is clear.

Our person, let us call her Sally, knows she will act unethically in order to protect those who cannot protect themselves, provided it will not put her kids at risk or make those she cares about ashamed. If Sally chooses to start an entrepreneurial venture, one with an ultimate goal of helping people get out of a "criminal lifestyle" by helping them start their own legal entrepreneurial venture, she is putting herself at risk for acting unethically, even if she does not realize it. You may ask how this can be the case. Sally is only trying to help others by giving people a legal way out. Based on her values, however, the problem is she is very likely to act unethically for the following reasons. Her kids are never at risk. In addition, if she is caught acting unethically the people she cares about might actually be proud of her because it was for a good cause (helping those who cannot otherwise help themselves). Finally, because of her choice of venture, she has a high probability of having to act unethically because it is very likely she will have to deal with some very unethical people just to help those she is trying to save get out of the "lifestyle." In short, it is like someone whom is a recovering alcoholic opening a bar in order to help others learn to drink responsibly. Although the goal is pure, the daily temptation to drink is just too great. This is why it is so important to take steps to prevent unethical behavior long before it even becomes an issue.

Chapter 8: Ethics and the Entrepreneur

Preventing Unethical Behavior

Based on our discussion, at this point it should be apparent why the only real way to avoid unethical behavior is to stay as far away as possible from the circumstances that can cause you to act unethically. Now that you understand this concept, it is possible to begin the process of trying to prevent unethical behavior.

Virtually every decision one makes in life has ethical consequences. The problem is most of the time we never take these consequences seriously. This is because at that moment it seems so unlikely that our decision would cause us to act unethically that it never even crosses our minds that we should put certain measures in place to make sure we will not be at risk of acting unethically. In the rest of our lives, it may not even be necessary. This is due to the built-in protection we have with our family, friends, acquaintances, and even bosses. These people all act to ensure the risk of acting unethically is minimal, as they will step in to let us know when we are at risk. However, we often forget that the moment we step into the role of entrepreneur, most often all these natural protections disappear. Primarily because we are entering territory that the people in our lives cannot help with, they have no way of knowing what we are doing at any given time and consequently cannot help steer us clear of the pitfalls. Therefore, entrepreneurs must be proactive when it comes to setting up ways of preventing unethical behavior.

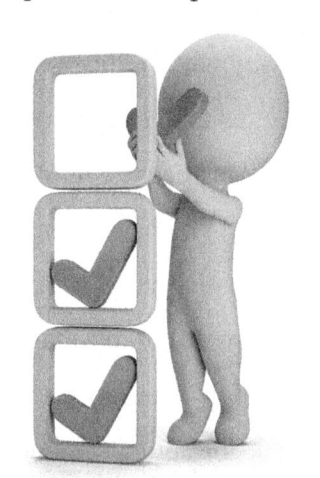

Checks and Balances

As previously mentioned, one of the main problems, from an ethical perspective that is, is that everyone starts to agree with everything you say once they begin to consider you a successful entrepreneur. Although this is amazing for the ego, this is a real problem when it comes to counting on others to let you know when you are at risk for acting unethically. Even if they see it coming, they assume that you know what you are doing and are going to continue to believe that up until the last minute. The problem is that entrepreneurs most often expect that if they were really at risk for acting unethically, someone around them would speak up. Unfortunately, this is not the case. There are three ways I know of to reduce the risk of acting unethically.

First, entrepreneurs need to find people who will tell them the truth, not what they want to hear. After all, with all that entrepreneurs go through to start an entrepreneurial venture the last thing they may want it someone who questions everything you do. Nevertheless, it is the smartest move an entrepreneur can make. On the way up, almost everyone is a naysayer and yes, it gets old quick. However, this is also the reason that most entrepreneurs made so many of the good decisions that they did. Everyone is always questioning what entrepreneurs are planning to do and it forces them to look at every decision to make sure that it is in fact the right one. The best thing to do, once entrepreneurs become successful, is to find that person or people who will not hold back. The ones who will tell you how they really feel regardless of what you want to hear and will ask questions, and keep asking questions, until it makes sense to them. They can be employees, family members, friends, anyone whom the entrepreneur can trust to give honest feedback no matter what. In this way, entrepreneurs can be sure that they are not selling themselves on a bad idea or course of action that in the end may put them at risk of acting unethically.

Another way to reduce the risk of acting unethically is the use of what I call a transparency test. Put quite simply, "Would those closest to you approve of what you are planning to do?" Application of this can take place in one of two ways. 1) By actually

Chapter 8: Ethics and the Entrepreneur

asking those people the entrepreneur cares about to give honest feedback on how they would feel if the entrepreneur were to follow the proposed course of action. Especially, if the whole world will know about it. This is sure to let any entrepreneur know if something is above board. 2) By entrepreneurs simply asking themselves what they believe these people would feel. Although this is a quicker way of doing it, it is also less accurate as it is dependent on how well the entrepreneurs actually know their people and how honest they are capable of being with themselves. The final way I know of to reduce the risk of acting unethically is to use what I call an empathy test. This is simply entrepreneurs trying to put themselves in place of those who will be affected by the proposed decision. Quite simply, "How would I feel if it were me or someone I care about?"

Although no measure will ensure that one is 100% ethical 100% of the time, the information here is the best way I know to reduce to a minimum the risk of acting unethically.

Section 3

Nascent Entrepreneurship

In the last section, we focused on the specifics of what makes an entrepreneur unique and what you need to do to prepare yourself for becoming an entrepreneur, the *how of becoming an entrepreneur*. Now we can shift our focus to nascence, or the *how entrepreneurs do what they do*.

In the past, we have used the term **nascent entrepreneur** to refer to a person who is preparing to become an entrepreneur for the first time. In contrast, the term **nascent entrepreneurship** refers to a person who is preparing to exploit a specific entrepreneurial opportunity for the first time. This is an important distinction because it can be either a nascent entrepreneur (first-timer) or an existing entrepreneur (old-timer). Nascent entrepreneurship effectively covers everything potential and existing entrepreneurs do prior to the actual exploitation of an opportunity. In essence, it covers all the prep work.

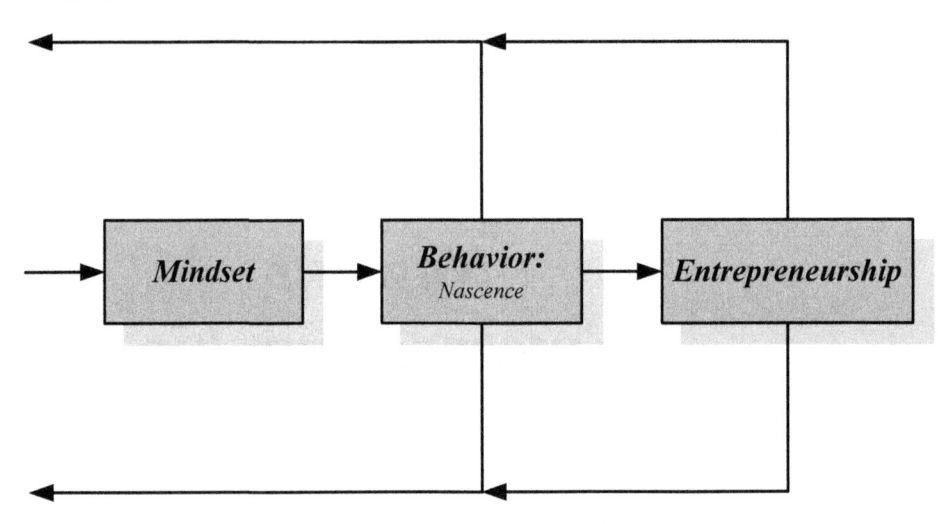

Mindset → *Behavior: Nascence* → *Entrepreneurship*

Section 3 focuses on how entrepreneurs do what they do, so that, when you are ready to become an entrepreneur, you will know where to begin. It is important to understand that Section 3 is but an overview of how entrepreneurs do what they do. It is *not everything you need to know* on each of the topics. In fact, for most of the chapters that follow, there are entire books devoted two several of the topics. To continue, Chapter 9 summarizes how entrepreneurs locate and create entrepreneurial opportunities. Chapter 10 addresses how one should evaluate the entrepreneurial opportunities located or created.

Chapter 9:

Locating and Creating Entrepreneurial Opportunities

One of the first questions asked of those who know entrepreneurship is typically, "How did you find your entrepreneurial opportunity?" Unfortunately, the most common answer is at best vague (luck, skill, I have a gift, etc.). In this chapter we will discuss the specifics of how entrepreneurs locate or create their entrepreneurial opportunities.

Locating and Creating Entrepreneurial Opportunities

Entrepreneurial opportunities are all around us. Nevertheless, the biggest problem facing most people who have chosen an entrepreneurial path, tends not to be money but the location or creation of an entrepreneurial opportunity that is right for them. Typically, this is because most people do not spend all their time looking and listening for entrepreneurial opportunities. Entrepreneurs, on the other hand, tend to be looking and listening for opportunities at all times. In fact, once you understand how to locate or create entrepreneurial opportunities, it becomes almost second nature—just like driving a car.

There are three primary ways of locating or creating entrepreneurial opportunities. They are *opportunity alertness* (often referred to simply as alertness), *constrained systematic search*, and a method I call *opportunity conversion*. It is through these three methods that the vast majority of all entrepreneurial opportunities are either located or created. It is important to note that each of these methods comes with its own, unique set of strengths and weaknesses.

Opportunity Alertness

Entrepreneurial alertness is a set of perceptual and mental processing skills that allows entrepreneurs to locate entrepreneurial opportunities[1,2] that others may not—

---

[1] Kirzner, I.M. (1978). *Competition and Entrepreneurship*. Chicago: University of Chicago Press.
[2] Kirzner, I.M. (1979). *Discovery and the Capitalist Process*. Chicago: University of Chicago Press

opportunity alertness. Alertness is what most (*untrained*) potential entrepreneurs use to locate their first opportunity. The process is really quite simple. Every problem that exists has the potential to be an entrepreneurial opportunity, and most people love to tell you their problems. To that end, all you really need to do is listen for any one of four simple opportunity phrases, "I wish," "I want," "I need," "I hate" (perceptual) and figure out a way to solve that problem (mental processing). The problem is that most of us have stopped listening. After all, who wants to listen to other people's problems, right? Guess what, entrepreneurs do. Entrepreneurs, however, do not try to solve every problem that comes their way.

Each of us has a unique set of knowledge and skills. Entrepreneurs quickly look at a problem and compare it to their knowledge and skill set to determine if they have the tools to address the problem. If they do not possess the tools, then they discard the problem and move on, leaving it for another entrepreneur to deal with. If they feel they may possess the tools to solve the problem, they will typically note it for further investigation later. *They note it for later*, this is important.

I cannot begin to tell you the number of great ideas I have located only to lose them because I did not write them down. In fact, every entrepreneur I have ever talked with has made the same mistake in the beginning. The reason we make the mistake of not writing it down is the idea seemed so great, and unique, that we thought there was just no way that we could ever forget it. Trust me when I tell you, you WILL lose even the greatest of ideas if you do not make a note of them in some form (pen and paper, audio recording, text message on your phone, email it to yourself, etc.). The best way I have found is simply to jot down a *name* (especially if you have a great name for it) and a *short description*, just enough so you would be able to know what you were talking about if you were not to look at it for a year or so. This we will call your *opportunity log*.

The *strength* of opportunity alertness is that many of the ideas located truly have the potential to be entrepreneurial opportunities, as opposed to business opportunities.

There are *weaknesses* to opportunity alertness. In most cases, individuals do not currently possess the knowledge, skills, social resources (contacts), and/or financial resources needed to act on most of the entrepreneurial opportunities located. This makes the length of time it takes to find an opportunity that is right for them unknowable. It could be anywhere from minutes to never, and a matter of luck. Although the more knowledge and skills one has, the more tools one has to work with, and the more potential problems one can potentially solve. Additionally, a problem with alertness is that most ideas located are business opportunities rather than entrepreneurial opportunities. This brings us to the second method of locating and creating entrepreneurial opportunities.

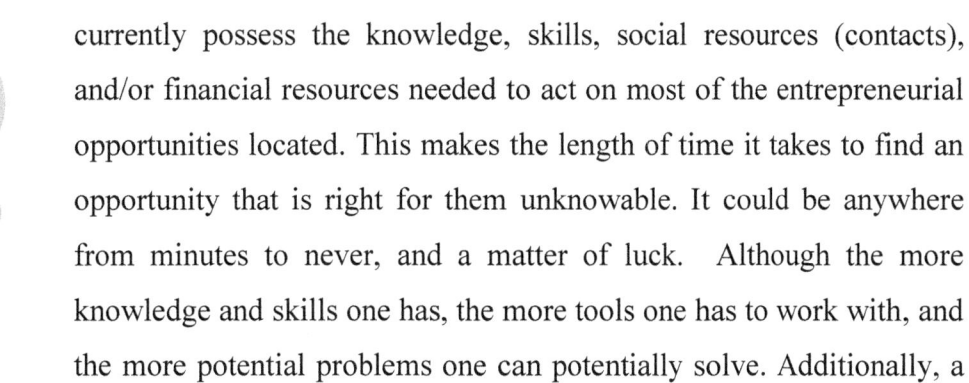

Just a note: *Based on my knowledge and research, it is my opinion that one of the main reasons so many entrepreneurs fail is because they grew tired of waiting for an opportunity to come along and tried to do something they were not suited for.*

Please do not make this mistake.

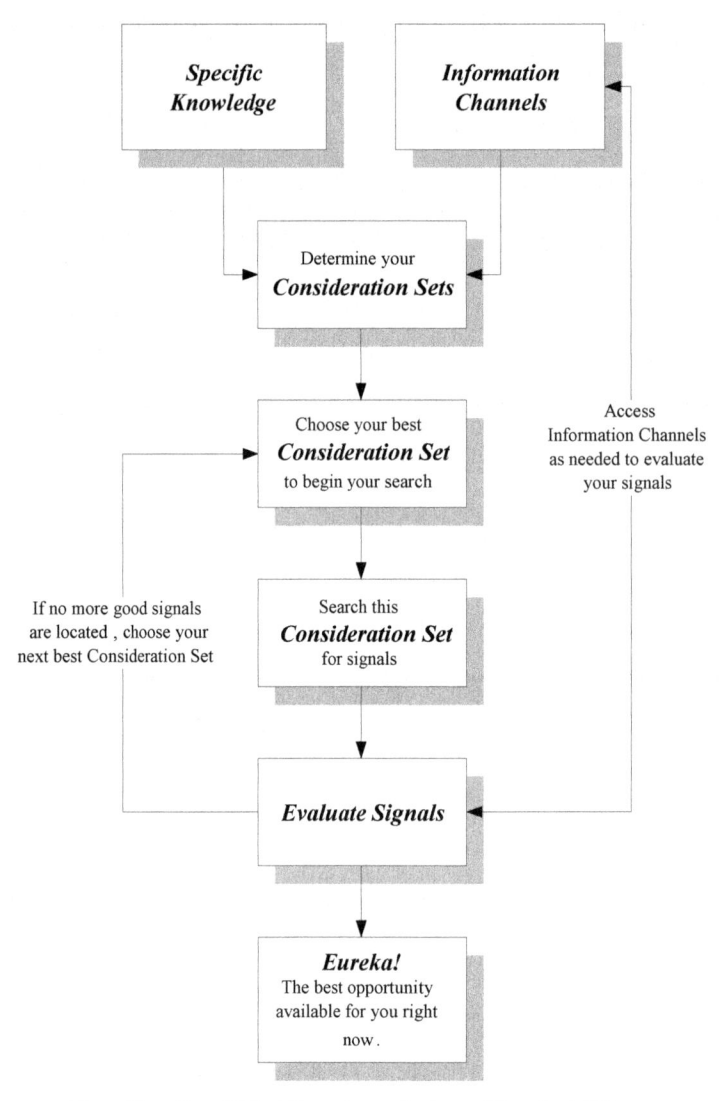

```
┌─────────────┐     ┌─────────────┐
│  Specific   │     │ Information │
│  Knowledge  │     │  Channels   │
└──────┬──────┘     └──────┬──────┘
       │                   │
       ↓                   │
   ┌───────────────┐       │
   │ Determine your│       │
   │Consideration Sets│◄───┤
   └───────┬───────┘       │
           ↓               │
   ┌───────────────┐       │
   │Choose your best│      │   Access
   │Consideration Set│     │ Information Channels
   │to begin your search│  │ as needed to evaluate
   └───────┬───────┘       │   your signals
           ↓               │
   ┌───────────────┐       │
   │  Search this  │       │
   │Consideration Set│     │
   │  for signals  │       │
   └───────┬───────┘       │
           ↓               │
   ┌───────────────┐       │
   │Evaluate Signals│◄─────┘
   └───────┬───────┘
           ↓
   ┌───────────────┐
   │   Eureka!     │
   │The best opportunity│
   │available for you right│
   │     now.      │
   └───────────────┘
```

If no more good signals are located, choose your next best Consideration Set

Adapted from Fiet, 2007, A Prescriptive Analysis of Search and Discovery

Constrained Systematic Search[3]

Constrained systematic search is an alternative method by which entrepreneurial opportunities can be located. Use of this method ensures that opportunities located are ones that individuals can pursue in the near future, if not now. It allows entrepreneurs,

---

[3] Fiet, J.O. (2008). *Prescriptive Entrepreneurship*. Boston: Edward Elgar Publishing.

and aspiring entrepreneurs, to improve search effectiveness by locating more opportunities, that they can actually pursue, in a shorter amount of time, than alertness. **Constrained systematic search** works on the premise that by constraining, or limiting, our search to areas where we possess a sufficient amount of knowledge, skills, and social resources we will locate or create a greater number of entrepreneurial opportunities we can actually act on.

As mentioned earlier, reports show that it is possible that as many as 90% of entrepreneurs start their first venture based on a previous job or their general knowledge of a particular industry. This is because it affords them a greater understanding of the *environment in which the business will function* (customers, suppliers, competitors, etc.), the *likely requirements for starting the venture* (number and kinds of employees needed, licensing, insurance, value of location, advertizing, etc.), and the *potential personal demands* (time, effort, stress, etc.). By choosing an opportunity based on such specific knowledge, potential entrepreneurs are able to reduce the risk associated with starting an entrepreneurial venture, thereby increasing their odds of success by ensuring that the fit between their knowledge, their social resources, and the venture idea is a good one.

Knowledge is the accumulation of understanding acquired through prior experience, education, and training. Such knowledge exists in two forms—general and specific.

General knowledge is acquired through sources such as basic education, books, magazines, the internet, television, or any source that is readily available to everyone. Easily transferred, this form of knowledge is transmitted to others with minimal effort or cost and therefore cannot be a sustained source of competitive advantage or wealth. General knowledge works to streamline

Chapter 9: Locating and Creating Entrepreneurial Opportunities

information, allowing for the creation of rules or guidelines that are easily applied, which in turn affords quick and easy evaluation of basic components of opportunities (e.g., determining current freight or component costs on the internet).

Specific knowledge is acquired through a person's life experiences, such as on-the-job training, job-related experience, specialized education, hobbies, friends, family, acquaintances, or any source that is not readily available to everyone. For that reason, specific knowledge is not easily transferable to others (they would have to live the same life to have the same specific knowledge), and therefore represents a potentially sustainable source of competitive advantage and wealth. It is important to understand that although *all specific knowledge is based on prior experience, not all prior experience is specific knowledge.* Specific knowledge is unique to the person and while others may possess some of the same knowledge, none will possess the exact same knowledge. This unique combination of knowledge allows a person to locate real entrepreneurial opportunities.

For example, a real estate developer who decides to return to college may discover an opportunity to develop student housing where none previously existed. This opportunity would likely have been discovered through the following knowledge: 1) the person's knowledge of building apartment complexes; 2) the knowledge of an impending need for student housing; and 3) the general knowledge that the college has no plans, funds, or ability to add student housing to the campus (known from an article in the student newspaper). While a significant number of people individually may know all three pieces of this information, few, if any, possess all three pieces other than the potential entrepreneur.

Information channels are any source of specific knowledge not held personally, but which the individual can access. Most information channels consist of associations with restricted access, such as memberships (clubs, organizations, etc.), written or electronic information that is difficult to locate or navigate (restricted books, manuals, websites, etc.), magazines that focus on specialized information (trade publications, etc.), and people. For example, while Matt knows nothing about cars, his sister Donna, being a master mechanic, represents an information channel for him regarding automotive matters. This information channel is unique due to a personal association. Other information channels may be available to everyone, but are unique due to the knowledge needed to access them. An information channel for real estate could be a real-estate office that has information about the number, size, cost, and location of houses for a given area or a contractor who knows how much it will cost to repair a rundown property. Other possible examples could be your inner circle of friends, family, business associates, the U.S. Patent Office, trade publications, trade shows, and the like.

The key difference between specific knowledge and information channels is who actually possesses the knowledge. Specific knowledge is information you have gathered from experience; information channels, in essence, are the specific knowledge of others that you have not yet learned but have the ability to access. Therefore, the most valuable information channels are the ones that others cannot access. With one's knowledge and information channels, one can use these resources to locate general areas where an accumulation of knowledge and information channels exists. These are consideration sets.

A **consideration set** is a promising grouping of knowledge and information channels that a person possesses which offers a high potential for the location of entrepreneurial opportunities.

For example, Tom previously worked for a landscaping company. His job was to prepare the soil for planting; removing grass, loosening the soil, etc. (specific knowledge). Tom also knows several agricultural farmers—experts on growing large numbers of plants, a horticulturist—an expert on specialized plants, and a zoologist—an expert on animals (information channels). These, when considered together, are a consideration set (we could call this set "Nature," although it is not critical that the set have a name).

Tom currently works for a manufacturing company that produces plastic containers. His job is to take plastic sheets and form them into containers using a machine (specific knowledge). His father and sister are mechanics; they can fix or make almost anything mechanical (information channels). Additionally, Tom is taking night classes to learn engineering. Because of these classes, Tom is learning how to design equipment and create blueprints (specific knowledge), and has access to a great number of technical manuals and several highly knowledgeable instructors in the field of mechanical engineering (information channels). Again, if we consider these as a whole, these represent another consideration set (for simplicity's sake we will call this set "Mechanical").

Thus, based on the amount of varying knowledge Tom has, and the number of people Tom knows who possess specific knowledge he does not, Tom may be able to create several more consideration sets. Such additional consideration sets could be based on other work experience, hobbies, or club memberships—anything that Tom has a sufficient amount of specific knowledge and information channels to support a search for opportunities. Opportunities do not have signs stating their existence. Nor do they come knocking on your door. You must search for them. This is what your consideration sets are for.

Signals. You begin by searching your consideration set for clues or **signals** that an opportunity exists. At this point, you are not looking for fully formed opportunities, simply signals that may represent a potential opportunity. Remember, the more obvious or easy to find the signal, the less valuable the opportunity is likely to be since others can likely see it too. Still, do not ignore an idea just because it was easy to locate. It is possible you were able to locate an opportunity easily because you possess a high degree of specific knowledge, and if few others possess this knowledge, it can still be extremely valuable.

Once you have located a signal, it is crucial that you write it down in your opportunity log just like, and even alongside, those located using alertness. This leads to the inevitable question, "when should I stop looking for opportunities?" The best answer is, "when you can answer yes to each of the following questions."

- *Have you thought hard about all your alternatives?*
- *Would you be satisfied with one of your existing ideas?*
- *Do you have a reasonable number of ideas from which to choose?*
- *Are some opportunities distinctly different from the others?*
- *Would it be unproductive to spend more time searching for ideas?*

If the answer to each of these questions is yes, then it is time to stop looking and start evaluating the ideas to determine how many represent viable opportunities (this is covered in the next chapter as it applies to all methods).

Chapter 9: Locating and Creating Entrepreneurial Opportunities

The *strengths* of systematic search are that it affords one the ability to locate more viable potential opportunities in a shorter period. Additionally, it likely reduces the rate of failure because the only opportunities located are ones for which the individual has knowledge and access to the information necessary to succeed.

The *weakness* of systematic search is that it suffers from the same problem as alertness, the location of primarily business opportunities rather than entrepreneurial opportunities. Nevertheless, each has value and both offer potential ideas for use with the next method, the creation of entrepreneurial opportunities.

Opportunity Conversion

Opportunity conversion is taking one or more conventional business opportunities and turning them into an entrepreneurial opportunity. In our discussion of creativity in Chapter 6 we hit on two psychological concepts that one can use to create new and unique opportunities from existing business opportunities. These are *divergent thinking* and *conceptual blending*, which are in essence combining unrelated concepts and objects into something new. In our case, we are talking about previously unrelated business ideas and opportunities. Let me give you an example of how it works.

Opportunity Log			
Name	**Description**	**BUS or ENT**
Flipping Houses	Buy the worst house in a great area, fix it up and rent or sell	BUS
Cupboard Organizer	Make custom shelving for inside existing cabinets	BUS
Green Housing Audit	Evaluate old homes and make recommendations on what to do to become more energy efficient	ENT ?
Interior Decorator	Bring the interior of older home into the modern era	BUS
Recondition Cars	Take old cars, fix them up	BUS
Customize Cars	Take existing cars and make them one of a kind	BUS
All American	A restaurant that serves American food	BUS

If we go back to our opportunity log and look at the ideas we have located, we can quickly see that most of the ideas we have located using opportunity alertness and constrained systematic search are business ideas. If this is the case with yours, do not despair, this is where opportunity conversion comes into play. Now remember the reason we want entrepreneurial over business opportunities is that business opportunities only offer an average return on investment (ROI) because of competition. Entrepreneurial opportunities, on the other hand, offer above average ROI since it takes time for competition to catch up, if they even can catch up (patents, copyrights, etc.).

First, take two completely different opportunities and try to put them together, the greater the difference the better. Do not worry if at first you cannot see how they could possibly go together, if it were easy someone else would have done it already. Let us start with the restaurant and customizing cars. Now the first ideas are most likely something like a catering service or a food truck. However, these already exist so we need to try harder. A full size, sit down, restaurant on wheels (*that is crazy— but possible*).

Take a semi trailer and modify it as they do mobile homes, with sides that slide out, and you could triple the size to approximately 24 x 50 feet. That is big enough for a full size, sit down restaurant. Take it to places where large numbers of people will be spending all or most of the day (maybe even the weekend) and set up (concerts, football games, festivals, etc.). If we choose the right events, we could charge an above average price and make a lot of money. Although this idea is difficult, it is possible. This is because we have the skills and the equipment from the auto body shop to make the trailer ourselves and we have the knowledge and expertise to set up and run a restaurant. This unique combination of knowledge, skills, and abilities is what makes it difficult and expensive for others to copy. Although this idea is possible, there is no reason to stop there. The best thing is to come up with as many ideas as possible, so let us try another.

A combination restaurant/auto body shop (*getting better*), a glass wall between the two would allow customers to check and see for themselves how repairs or customization of their car was coming while they eat. You would make money as they visit the restaurant to see the progress of the work done on their car. People having custom work done would likely eat at the restaurant almost on a weekly basis and bring their friends. Furthermore, custom work can take up to a year or more to complete and some people would eat there just because they love to see custom cars being born.

Opportunity Log		
Name	**Description**	**BUS or ENT**
Flipping Houses	Buy the worst house in a great area, fix it up and rent or sell	BUS
Cupboard Organizer	Make custom shelving for inside existing cabinets	BUS
Green Housing Audit	Evaluate old homes and make recommendations on what to do to become more energy efficient	ENT?
Interior Decorator	Bring the interior of older home into the modern era	BUS
Recondition Cars	Take old cars, fix them up	BUS
Customize Cars	Take existing cars and make them one of a kind	BUS
All American	A restaurant that serves American food	BUS
Traveling Restaurant	A mobile, sit down restaurant that serves American food	ENT
Check out my car	A Restaurant/Auto body shop (glass wall in between)	ENT

Although we are going to stop here, you should be able to see how one can keep going. The key is to take as many of your business opportunities as possible and combine (convert) them into something new and unique—*an entrepreneurial opportunity*.

The *strength* of opportunity conversion is that it affords one the ability to take existing business opportunities one has located (average ROI) and convert them into entrepreneurial opportunities (above average ROI).

The *weakness* of opportunity conversion is that it often requires one to have a great deal of knowledge, skills, and experiences from which to draw. Therefore, it may be difficult for potential entrepreneurs who are younger, and thus have less diverse knowledge, skills, and experiences to draw from, to use.

Now that we have an understanding of how entrepreneurs locate and create entrepreneurial opportunities, it is time to look at how entrepreneurs evaluate, or should evaluate, their opportunities.

Chapter 10:

Evaluating Opportunities

The focus of this chapter is to understand how entrepreneurs evaluate, or should evaluate, opportunities quickly in order to determine the best opportunity for them to pursue right now.

Opportunity Fit

To begin any discussion on evaluating opportunities, it is first necessary to understand there is far more that should go into a life changing commitment like entrepreneurship than financial return on investment (ROI). What is as important, or may be even more important than ROI, is the degree to which the opportunity fits the entrepreneur and their lifestyle. Fit is often thought to be the degree to which an individual possesses the understanding required to exploit an opportunity. In this case, fit is the knowledge, experience, training, or any such ability required to bring a specific opportunity to realization. In essence, does the entrepreneur know what they need to know? Too often, this is considered the standard for how well an opportunity fits an entrepreneur. The problem is there is much more to return on investment than money. In fact, for most entrepreneurs, money primarily acts only as a measure of success (after they achieve a reasonable base income of course). Therefore, there are other considerations of fit that must be taken into account.

The four major considerations of any opportunity are...
1. *Monetary value*, does the opportunity offer enough monetary rewards to make it worth pursuing (financial ROI)?
2. *Personal knowledge*, do you know, or have the connections to find out, what it will really take to pursue the opportunity?
3. *Personal value, w*ill you be content managing the opportunity day in and out? If not, will you be able to sell it (personal ROI)?
4. *Family value, ca*n your personal life survive the pursuit of the opportunity (family ROI)?

To put these into terms you may be more familiar with, we could group them another way. **Feasibility**, which is in essence, *should it be done* (monetary fit) and *can you do it* (personal knowledge), and, **desirability** *will you enjoy doing it indefinitely* (personal value) and *will your family/friends be proud of you for doing it* (family value). For now we will stick to the four separate groupings.

In order to ensure that an opportunity is a good fit, the four of these must be taken into consideration. If any one of the four is extremely low, the opportunity may represent more unhappiness than happiness. This does not mean that such an opportunity has no value. It simply means that one either needs to take steps to improve the low score before pursuing the opportunity, or one should consider partnering with someone who is a better fit in that area. Additionally, one always has the option of selling the idea. In any case, a good opportunity is a good opportunity; it all comes down to determining the best way to exploit it and still be happy with the outcome. The following is an example of a scorecard that could be used to ensure that all four areas are given proper consideration in evaluating an opportunity and its fitness.

Opportunity Scorecard

Name	Monetary Value Fit	Personal Knowledge Fit	Personal Value Fit	Family Value Fit	Opportunity Score

Confirmation Bias

Before we begin a discussion of how entrepreneurs value, or should value, the different value-fit considerations, it is important that we discuss a concept that has a significant effect on any decision—confirmation bias.

Confirmation bias is one's tendency to favor information that confirms one's beliefs and to devalue or ignore information that does not. In essence, confirmation bias is the tendency to favor information that supports the opportunities we like and to ignore (or discount) any information that does not. Due to this bias, it is crucial that one set up some objective (unbiased) measures for most of the value-fit areas before beginning to evaluate any opportunities.

Determining Monetary Value-Fit (Feasibility)

Monetary value-fit has two components that entrepreneurs need to take into account. First, the traditional and most obvious is **profit potential**. How much money can one reasonably expect to make from the opportunity, and for how long? The second consideration is **opportunity cost**, is it worth giving up the next best thing (usually one's current job) to pursue the opportunity?

Creating an Objective Measure of Profit Potential

One way to attempt to remove confirmation bias from the value-fit evaluation is to predetermine an objective measure of profit potential. Because profit potential is most likely related to current income, let us begin there. You might say, "as long as I make more than I'm making now, I'd do it." The problem with this thinking is you are likely not taking into account all the benefits that come with your current source of income. What about the current benefits (life and health insurance, retirement, job security, a steady paycheck, etc.)? Therefore, in order for an opportunity to be a good value-fit, it must offer more than a little more than what you are making now. It must offer enough income to cover all the things you will have to pay for yourself that your current employer has been paying for.

Chapter 10: Evaluating Opportunities

The best means I have found for creating an objective measure of profit potential is to take what you earn now, and add in how much your benefits will cost for you to provide them yourself. These include, health insurance, vacation benefits, and even retirement contributions. For example, let us say you are currently making $25,000 per year and your employer offers health insurance, life insurance, and a retirement contribution. If you have a family that is counting on your income and health insurance to survive, you need to find out how much health insurance would be and add that in. Just to give you an idea, the average cost of family health insurance in 2013 was $6,000 per year for an individual and $16,000 per year for a family. Therefore, you would need at least $41,000 ($25,000 + $16,000) just to make do if you have a family, and we are not done yet. If your company contributes to your retirement (say 5%), now you need to add in an additional $1,250.

Another consideration that most potential entrepreneurs do not take into account is what if something goes wrong. Did you know that in many states, an entrepreneur is only given a maximum of 8 weeks unemployment no matter how long they were in business (none if you are not in business long enough)? Therefore, if something goes wrong, entrepreneurs need to have money to cover their bills until they can find another job. The best rule of thumb, to be safe, is six months. That means taking your bare minimum to survive without falling behind on your payments (i.e., $1,500), times six, and adding that into your minimum total. As a result, for our example, $51,250 is the least amount you would want to make in yearly profit to consider quitting your job to pursue this opportunity.

Once one has a minimum, the next step is to calculate a maximum. This is the amount that one would be willing to quit their current job (today) for in order to pursue the opportunity. The tendency is to use an outrageous maximum number (such as $1,000,000) although in reality it is usually much lower than you might think. Think of it this way, what amount, realistically, would you be willing to drop everything for to pursue an opportunity? A good rule of thumb is five times your minimum. So, for the above example, it would be approximately $256,250. Now for the other end of the scale, the minimum amount for which one would waste any time on in any way, shape, or form (i.e., a hobby, part-time for extra cash, etc.). In this instance, you have to consider what your free time is worth. This is because the pursuit of an opportunity, no matter how small, will take you away from some of the things you like to do. I would use a number somewhere between $2,500 and $25,000, but you have to determine this based on your own life.

With these three numbers determined, it is now possible to create an objective measure. My preference is a scale of 0 to 10, but use whatever graduations you feel most comfortable using. The one thing you have to keep in mind is that all of the measures used for the four different *fits* must ultimately use the same scale. To create the measure, simply create an index with 11 spots numbered 0 through 10. Put your maximum take no action number in the zero spot (we will use $10,000 for this example). Next, put your minimum number for which you would consider pursuing an opportunity right now in the number five spot ($51,250 in our example). Finally, use your maximum number, the one for which you would drop everything and pursue an opportunity right now, in the number ten spot (again, in our example that would be $256,250). If you decide to use a 1 – 5 scale then these numbers would go in the 1, 3, and 5 spots respectively. Now, we can use simple math to fill in the blanks in between these numbers with evenly graduated numbers.

The following is an example.

Graduations between #5 and #10

$$\frac{256{,}250 - 51{,}250}{5} = 41{,}000$$

Graduations between 0 and #5

$$\frac{51{,}250 - 10{,}000}{5} = 8{,}250$$

Score	Yearly Profit
0	**$10,000**
1	$18,250
2	$26,500
3	$34,750
4	$43,000
5	**$51,250**
6	$92,250
7	$133,250
8	$174,250
9	$215,250
10	**$256,250**

Now that one has an objective measure of monetary value-fit, it is possible to estimate (objectively) the monetary value of potential opportunities located or created using any of the methods from Chapter 9.

Estimating the Monetary Value of an Opportunity

The best place to start when estimating the value of a given opportunity is yearly profit. To *estimate yearly profit*, first determine the cost to produce or provide a single unit. If it is a product, make sure you include shipping cost, handling cost, production cost, etc. If it is a service, make sure you take into account transportation, supplies, etc. In either case, the idea is to include anything that goes into or is used up during the creation of the product or when providing the service. Next, add in 30% to 50% of the selling price for markup to cover the overhead (monthly expenses such as rent, computers, stationery, internet, etc.); the amount is dependent on the industry you are supplying. For example, in the manufacturing industry the standard markup is 15%, in the apparel market it can be 70% or more. This is where specific knowledge and information channels come into play. If you do not know the standard markup of your industry, go to your information channels for the information. Note, when in doubt—go high, better safe than sorry. Once completed you have an estimated unit cost; now you need a selling price.

Selling price is, in essence, what most people would pay for the product or service you are planning to provide. If the price of the product or service is too high, no one will buy it. On the other hand, if the price is too low you will lose money. The key is to have the highest price that most people are willing to pay. This number is dependent on three factors. 1) **Rarity**, how easy is it for people to find your product or service. If they can only get it from you, you can charge more than if they can also get it from others. 2) **Inimitability**, how difficult is it for others to make the product or offer the service, and 3) **demand**, how bad people want it. All three are equally important and necessary to the determination of value. For example, say you have a product you wish to sell. It is extremely *rare* because you are the only one who makes anything like it. People you have shown it to fall in love with it and cannot wait to buy one (*demand*). However, the product is very easy to make and made from everyday materials you can find around the house (*not imitable*). In this case, the selling price would have to be extremely low (virtually no profit at all) or people would simply make it themselves. The same is true if any of the three factors are low.

Chapter 10: Evaluating Opportunities

If demand and inimitability are high, but the product is not rare, the price has to be low because people can get it anywhere. If the product is rare and inimitable, but there is no demand for the product, no one will want to buy it unless it is virtually free. This is why it is important to determine, at the very least, that the product or service that you are considering is moderately rare, inimitable, and there is going to be a reasonable demand for it. This will afford you at least the standard profit for the industry. The best situation is when the product or service you are looking to provide is high on all three. If the product or service is rare, extremely difficult to imitate (*inimitable*), and there is a tremendous demand for it, you will virtually be able to name your own price. Picture a car that runs on water and never wears out that only you know how to build and cannot be reverse engineered (taken apart to see how it was made). In this instance, you can charge any amount that people can afford; how about the cost of a house, or maybe even double that.

Once you have determined an estimated yearly profit, it is now important to determine the *estimated life of the opportunity*. Not every product or service lives forever. It is important this fact is taken into account when determining the monetary value of an opportunity. For example, a new application (app) for a computer is only good until the next generation of computers comes out (typically five to seven years). Once the next generation is here, your app stops working and your sales decrease dramatically. What if your product is a onetime buy for people, say a can opener with a lifetime guarantee. While you may sell tons at first, once everyone buys one, sales will drop off to nothing. Worse, the product or service can be duplicated. As soon as you start making a lot of money, other companies will begin to produce a similar product or offer a similar service. Such competition will drive down your profit. Factors such as these must be taken into account when determining the monetary value of your opportunity. You do not want to choose an opportunity that, while great at first, will not last long enough to give you a good return on your investment (time and money).

One of the best ways to calculate the monetary value of an opportunity is to calculate the **unit cost** (how much will it cost to produce or provide) plus the **overhead** (how much does it cost to keep the doors open, rent, insurance, taxes, equipment cost, etc.) times industry **margin** (standard amount over cost and overheard). Next, you need to determine what you can reasonably sell the product or service for. When you subtract the two, you will have your profit per unit. Multiple your profit per unit by the number of units you can conservatively sell per year and you have your potential yearly profit. The last step is to multiply your yearly profit by the number of years until the product is obsolete and you have the total monetary value of the opportunity. Once you have this number, you can use the objective measure you created to rate the monetary value of the opportunity (i.e., 1 to 10, 1 to 5, etc.). While this process may seem quite complex, it is really just some simple math with a little bit if research thrown in. Take it one step at a time and in no time you will be doing it like a pro. Here is an example.

Opportunity:	Custom Jewelry
Cost per Unit:	Materials $5.00 + Assembly $2.00 + Shipping $1.50 = $8.50
Overhead:	Workspace $200/month + Insurance $50/month / 200 units made = $1.00
Industry Margin:	$8.50 + $1.00 = $9.50 * 70% margin = $16.15
Selling Price:	$25.00
Profit per Unit:	$25.00 - $16.15 = $8.85
Yearly Profit:	$8.85 * 2400 units per year = $21,240 (Based on the yearly profit this opportunity only rates a **2** on the scale)
Survival:	5 years until obsolescence (Based on the scale, this opportunity is at best a **part-time** one or a **hobby**)

Chapter 10: Evaluating Opportunities

Once you have this opportunity scored, simply move to the next opportunity on your list until you have created a monetary fit score for each of the opportunities you have located.

Determining Personal-Knowledge Fit (Feasibility)

Personal-knowledge fit is the degree to which an individual possesses the understanding required to exploit an opportunity. In this case, it is the knowledge, experience, training, or any such ability required to bring a specific opportunity to realization. Do you know what you need to know?

When evaluating an opportunity, the more you know about what it takes to bring a potential product or service to market, the more accurate the evaluation. Therefore, it is important to determine just how much knowledge, or access to information, is missing for each opportunity. The best way to determine this type of fit objectively is to determine what needs to be known and compare it to what you know or can easily find out.

The following is an example of one possible way to evaluate fit. In this example, the idea is to determine whether each of the items is necessary to bring the potential product or service to market by marking yes or no. Next, for every item marked yes, list if you *currently* know or *have a source* to find out the information and briefly list the source (me, John the contractor, etc.). Finally, total up the number of sources you have and divide by the number of requirements. This will give you a percentage of fit. For example, let us say your score is .538 (14 known or sources / 26 required). This suggests you *currently* know or have access to 54% of the information you need to pursue this

Discovering the Entrepreneur Within

opportunity. Thus on a scale of 1 to 10, the fit for this opportunity would then be a five.

Evaluation of Person-Knowledge Fit

Does this opportunity require ...	Yes	No	Have source	Source
Product / Service				
Design/Engineering	❏	❏	❏	
Outsource (someone to make it)	❏	❏	❏	
Equipment (machines to make it)	❏	❏	❏	
Licenses/permits	❏	❏	❏	
Patent, Copyright, or Trademark	❏	❏	❏	
Experience	❏	❏	❏	
Other:	❏	❏	❏	
Market				
Knowledge of the number of possible customers	❏	❏	❏	
Knowledge of the number of competitors	❏	❏	❏	
Knowledge of the market growth rate	❏	❏	❏	
Knowledge of long-term prospects (sustainability)	❏	❏	❏	
Knowledge of how much customers will pay	❏	❏	❏	
Knowledge of competitors' pricing	❏	❏	❏	
Knowledge of customer satisfaction with existing product or service	❏	❏	❏	
Other:	❏	❏	❏	
Business				
A legal entity (DBA, incorporation, etc.)	❏	❏	❏	
A physical location (building, office, etc.)	❏	❏	❏	
Furniture	❏	❏	❏	
Computers	❏	❏	❏	
Supplies	❏	❏	❏	
Vehicles	❏	❏	❏	
Advertising	❏	❏	❏	
Employees	❏	❏	❏	
Other:	❏	❏	❏	
Professional Services				
Lawyer – Contracts	❏	❏	❏	
Lawyer – Regulatory	❏	❏	❏	
Accountant – Taxes (Federal, State, Local)	❏	❏	❏	
Accountant – Payroll & Taxes	❏	❏	❏	
Insurance – Property	❏	❏	❏	
Insurance – Liability	❏	❏	❏	
Other:	❏	❏	❏	
	Total Requirements		*Total Sources*	

*** ***Score:*** *(Total Sources / Total Requirements) * 100 = Current Fit*

The preceding list is an example of one possible means of determining person-knowledge fit. Depending on whether you are evaluating a product or a service, and the type of opportunity, the list shown may vary dramatically. It is important that you make changes to the list according to the opportunity. You may end up with several different versions if you have several different types of opportunities.

Determining Personal-Value Fit (Desirability)

Personal value is the significance an opportunity has for you. Because this facet of opportunity evaluation is personal, only you can truly determine what aspects comprise the measure. In order to create a measure, start with evaluating the things that are most important to you in life. It is crucial you are honest with yourself. For example, if you really hate working for other people then freedom and control might be important aspects. On the other hand, if you enjoy structure and the safety of others making the decisions, then security might be an important aspect to you.

Look at it this way, if you were single, no family or friends, what would be important to you? This is important because family and friends are not around 24/7. Looking at what makes you truly happy, when no one else is around, is one way to figure out what is important to you. For example, a job you truly love might mean you need purpose in your life. Time to read or relax might indicate you value downtime, and so on. The only way to evaluate who you are is to examine what is truly important to you. These items should be on your list (do not use the following example, this is an example to give you some ideas, you MUST create your own list).

Personal-Value Fit

Important to me ...	Yes	No
Achievement		
Control		
Affiliation (belonging)		
Power		
Glory		
Conformity		
Freedom		

Once you have your list, use it to determine how well the opportunity fits what you are looking for in life. Total up the number of no's you have and divide by the number of yeses. This will again give you a percentage of fit, allowing you to convert easily to the 1 to 10 scale like the other fit measures. Remember, this could be a 1 to 5 scale, or even a percentage scale. What is important is that all the measures ultimately use the same scale.

Determining Family-Value Fit (Desirability)

Family-value fit is the most often overlooked measure of fit. For this measure, look at what is important to the people in your life that matter most to you. This is important because the requirements of a particular opportunity may conflict with what matters to those you care for. For example, if the opportunity requires you to be away from home for weeks at a time, and you have a spouse and children, it may reduce family-value fit. On the other hand, if you are single and have no real ties (family or friends) this measure plays no role in the evaluation of an opportunity. In this case, simply leave it blank.

Chapter 10: Evaluating Opportunities

Family-Value Fit

Will the opportunity allow me to ...	Yes	No
Spend enough time with my significant other		
Spend enough time with my kids		
Spend enough time with my other family members		
Spend enough time with my other friends		
Will my significant other be proud of what I am doing		
Will my kids be proud of what I am doing (Billy)		
Will my kids be proud of what I am doing (Suzy)		
Will my kids be proud of what I am doing (Tommy)		
Will my other family members be proud of what I am doing		
Will my friends be proud of what I am doing		

Once again, this list must be personalized to you based on those people in your life who care about you. An opportunity may affect your relationship with them. This is important because opportunities usually take more time and energy than expected and have a tendency to do so for far longer than expected. Ignoring, or not taking this measure, can have serious consequences on your personal life. Just keep in mind that it is meaningless to achieve everything you want in life if you end up having no one to share it with. The best way to complete this measure is simply to figure out what the effects of pursuing the opportunity are on the people around you and then ask them how they feel about it. But be honest, if you tell them it will only take you away for one year and it ends up being three, the answers you get are likely incorrect. You matter to them and they would often rather have you be a significant part of their life than the money you may be able to offer them if it works.

As you did with personal-value fit, once the family-value fit is complete, total up the number of no's you have and divide by the number of yeses. This will again give you a percentage of fit, allowing you to convert easily to the 1 to 10 scale like the other fit measures.

Overall Evaluation (Opportunity Score)

The final step in the process is to determine an opportunity score for each of the opportunities you have located. Again, how you created your opportunity scores is dependent on how you scored each of the four components of fit. Based on the previous examples, your opportunity scorecard should look something like this. However, not all measures of fit may be created equally. If your family-value (or any of the other measures) represents a significant consideration factor, then it may be necessary to weight that measure heavier. If this is the case, determine how much more it matters than the rest and adjust accordingly. For example, if family-value matters as much as all the other measures put together, simply multiply each number by 3 (in this example all fits are considered equal).

Opportunity Scorecard

Name	Monetary Value Fit	Personal Knowledge Fit	Personal Value Fit	Family Value Fit	Opportunity Score
Flipping Houses	4	2	5	6	17
Cupboard Organizer	6	2	8	4	18
Green Housing Audit	5	8	5	6	24
Interior Decorator	4	1	7	1	13
Recondition Cars	6	1	10	2	19
Customize Cars	5	3	7	4	19
All American	6	7	8	7	28
Traveling Restaurant	6	7	6	4	23
Check out my car	8	7	8	7	30

Now that you have scored all of your opportunities, the decision of what opportunities are worth further investigation is clear. In our example, the "All American" (#7) and "Check out my car" (#9) restaurants are both overall good. However, if the goal is to quit your current job as soon as possible, the "Check out

Chapter 10: Evaluating Opportunities

my car" restaurant is the better choice. It offers the best chance to make a living capable of monetarily supporting you and your family (see column 2).

Once an entrepreneur has narrowed down the opportunities to the best option (or options), it is time to create a detailed plan for exploiting them. This is the topic of the next chapter.

Note: It is extremely important that one understands that the method used for estimating monetary value is for narrowing down the opportunity pool only. In creating an entrepreneurial business plan, it will likely be necessary to complete a more detailed estimation for some areas of the plan.

Appendix A: Chapter Exercises

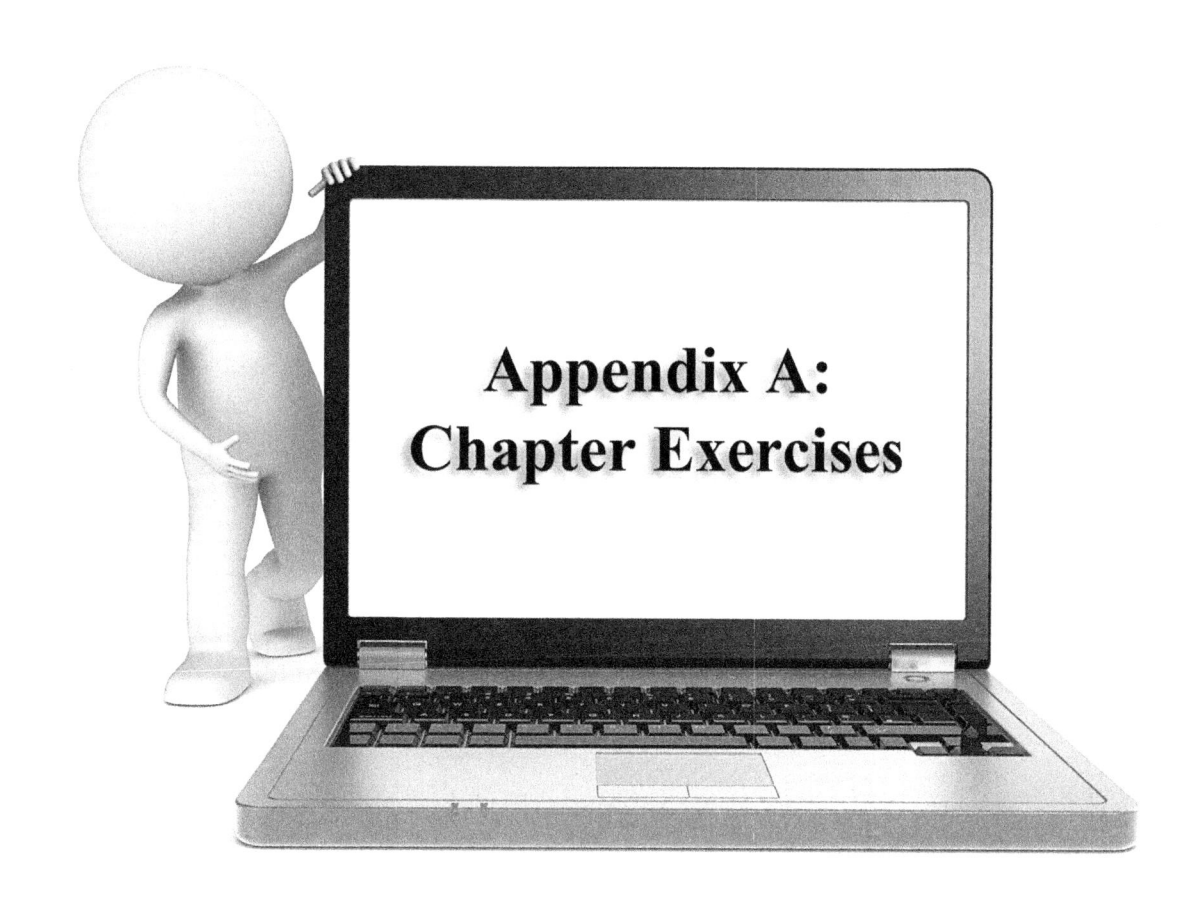

Exercise 1: Interview with an Entrepreneur

Locate an entrepreneur and schedule time to sit down and talk with them about how they got started and what they feel you should know before you begin your own entrepreneurial journey. Feel free to add more questions that you feel may be appropriate. *If you do not know or cannot locate any entrepreneurs, feel free to search for an interview that others have done (internet, television, etc).*

What made your entrepreneurial opportunity unique?

___

___

How much research did you do before you really started, and what kind?

___

___

How did you go about researching your opportunity?

___

___

If you could do it all over again—would you?

___

___

If you could do it all over again—what would you do differently?

___

___

What advice would you give to someone just getting started?

_____
_____

Additional questions of your own:

_____
_____
_____
_____
_____
_____
_____
_____
_____
_____
_____
_____
_____
_____
_____
_____
_____
_____
_____

Exercise 2: The Value of an Entrepreneurial Economy

Describe three specific examples that show the benefits of or the need for an entrepreneurial economy or society. These should be **current** stories taken from any reputable source (i.e. newspapers, books, news reports, etc). Make sure you attach some form of documentation to support the example (i.e. newspaper clipping, book name, website address, or anything that can be verified).

Economic Growth

_____
_____
_____
_____
_____

Employment Growth

_____
_____
_____
_____
_____

Employer-Employee Loyalty

_____
_____
_____
_____
_____

Exercise 3: Describe Which Path Is Right for You.

Based on what you have learned from the chapter, describe your entrepreneurial intentions, and, where you see yourself in the entrepreneurial process currently.

What are your entrepreneurial intentions and why.

_____
_____
_____

Based on your entrepreneurial intentions, when do think you would become an entrepreneur. Explain your thought process.

_____
_____
_____
_____
_____
_____

When are you most likely to begin the entrepreneurial process and why?

_____
_____
_____
_____
_____
_____

Appendix A: Chapter Exercises

Exercise 4: Which Form of Entrepreneurship Is Right for You?

Based on what you have learned from the chapter, describe which form of entrepreneurship you are most likely to undertake.

What form of entrepreneurship do you think you will choose and why?

___

Explain how you think this may happen and when.

___

Do you think you will choose to make your venture a social one, why or why not.

___

Appendix A: Chapter Exercises

Exercise 5: Forming Your Entrepreneurial Mindset

Based on what you have learned from the chapter, what specific areas do you need to work on in order to form, or strengthen, your entrepreneurial mindset and how will you begin to do so?

Entity Schema

Possible Self

Self-Efficacy

Exercise 6: Creativity and Innovation

Chapter 6 talked about a number of different methods for reinvigorating your creativity. Please list which methods, if any, you feel would best help you become a more creative person. *If you do not feel you need assistance with your creativity, describe in detail why you would not benefit from these techniques.*

Exercise 7: Psychological Hardiness

Based on chapter 7, write a 1-page summary, in letterform, explaining specifically what you are going to do to become a more psychologically hardy individual and when. Longer is acceptable just make sure you include discussions about the following topics.

1. Commitment as it related to psychological hardiness.
2. Cognitive, decisional, and behavioral control as it related to psychological hardiness.
3. Challenges as it related to psychological hardiness.
4. The importance of psychological hardiness to the entrepreneur

Exercise 8: Entrepreneurial Ethics

Chapter 8 described several situations that can cause an entrepreneur to be at risk for acting unethical. To combat this threat the chapter suggested listing ones core beliefs. In this assignment list your core beliefs and discuss what ethical dilemmas you might face based on these beliefs and how you can reduce the risk of acting unethically.

Core Beliefs

Potential Dilemmas

How you will avoid these potential dilemmas

Exercise 9: Locating and Creating Opportunities

Based on the different methods of locating and creating entrepreneurial opportunities listed in chapter 9, which do you feel is the best method for you and why.

Exercise 10: Evaluating Opportunities

It is now time to consider if your venture is feasible. Evaluate the following aspects of your future venture make sure you address each of these topics.

Monetary Value: can you make the venture profitable? Estimate the cost to produce – selling price = potential profitability. Explain how you came up with these numbers and why you feel they are accurate.

_____
_____
_____
_____
_____

Personal Knowledge: do you know, or can you find out, what you need to know to start your venture—explain.

_____
_____
_____
_____
_____

Personal Value: How well does the opportunity fit your needs personally?

_____
_____
_____
_____
_____

Family Value: What are the sacrifices you will have to make and are you able and willing (i.e. time with family, friends, hobbies, etc.)?

CPSIA information can be obtained
at www.ICGtesting.com
Printed in the USA
LVOW02s1210290416

485859LV00003B/8/P